Book 2

Enrichment Units in Math

Written by Dianne Draze & Judy Leimbach

Illustrated by Elisa Ahlin

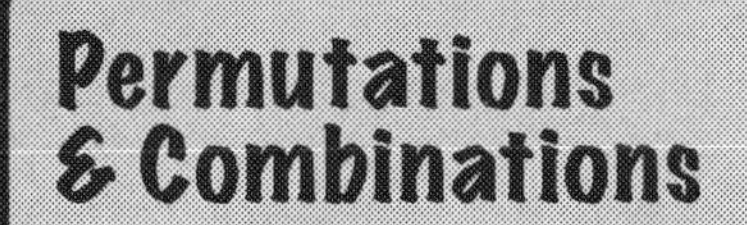

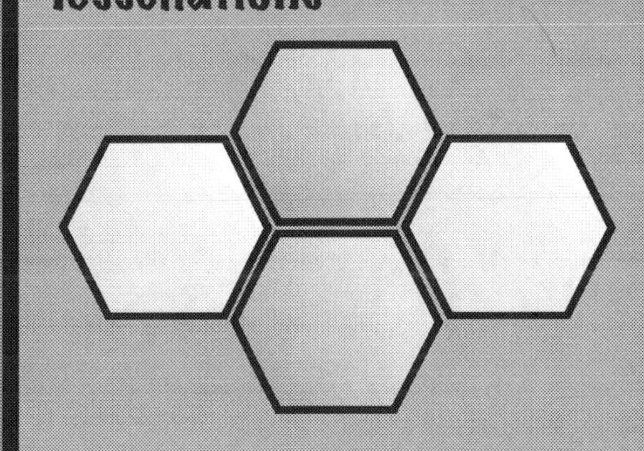

Line Drawings

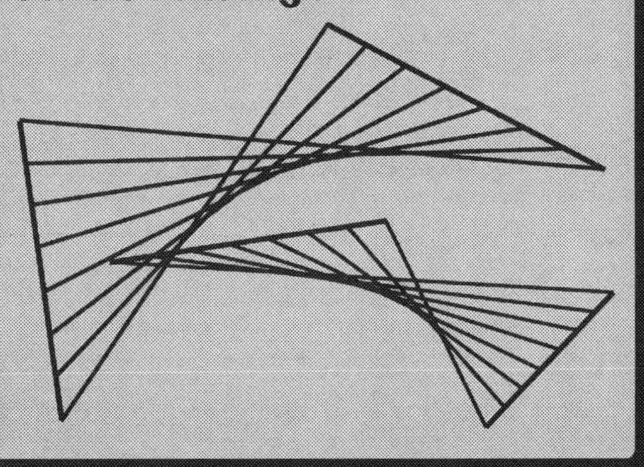

Graphing

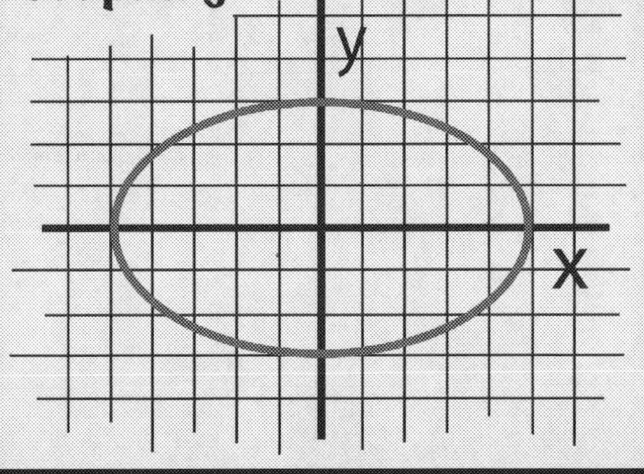

Contents

First published in 2005 by Prufrock Press Inc.

Published in 2021 by Routledge
605 Third Avenue, New York, NY 10017
2 Park Square, Milton Park, Abingdon, Oxon OX14 4RN

Routledge is an imprint of the Taylor & Francis Group, an informa business.

ISBN-13:978-1-5936-3069-0 (pbk)

DOI: 10.4324/9781003235026

Instructions for Teachers

Mathematics is more than simply performing computations or memorizing basic facts. It is present all around us, from the designs in granny's quilt to the patterns on our floors and walls. Mathematics is concerned with making sense of the world around us. Mathematical thinking helps us make connections, see order and think logically.

Our students should be provided with a variety of opportunities to explore mathematical ideas in ways that promote their intellectual growth and expand their views of what mathematics really is. This book provides four enrichment units that involve students actively and intellectually in mathematical thinking.

1. Line Designs

Line designs are created by straight lines, but because of the way these lines intersect, they produce a design that appears to have curved lines. This is a fun unit that will develop students' abilities to follow directions, measure, use geometric construction tools and visualize. Students like doing these designs because with only a little skill and perseverance, they can construct designs that are attractive. There are a multitude of designs that can be created using only the simple techniques that are presented in this book. Students should be encouraged to experiment with different geometric figures or to combine the geometric forms that are presented in this unit to make their own designs.

2. Combinations and Permutations

Combinations and permutations are concepts that are presented indirectly in many problems that students are asked to solve in their math classes. By introducing them to these two different ways of sorting items and by giving them strategies to determine how many different combinations are possible for each situation, we will have given them a tool that will simplify their future problem solving efforts. These two concepts are a prerequisite for solving probability problems.

3. Tessellations

Tessellation refers to the ability to cover a surface with flat tiles without any gaps between the tiles or without overlapping the tiles. Regular tessellations are composed of the same shape repeated over and over again. The only shapes that will form a regular tessellation are an equilateral triangle, a square and a hexagon. Students will not only learn about the basic concepts of tesselating, but will also learn several techniques for creating their own irregular tessellaitons. This unit involves visual thinking, geometry, and art. It is a unit that students enjoy, because, like line designs, they can create attractive designs. But don't be fooled by the fun factor – it's a unit that requires serious thinking and attention to detail as well as an understanding of geometric figures.

4. Coordinate Graphing

Students are routinely introduced to graphing as a way to organize data, but are less frequently introduced to coordinate graphing in the elementary grades. This unit introduces the concepts of number lines, positive and negative numbers, and coordinate graphs. This unit presents concepts that will be used later in the student's math career in geometry, algebra and calculus. The skills of identifying and plotting points on a coordinate graph are combined in an entertaining format of creating pictures, making this a motivating unit.

How to Use the Units

The materials in this book may be used as extension units for the whole class or as enrichment for individuals or small groups.

While all students should have opportunities to explore mathematical ideas and to go beyond practicing computational skills, for the able math students who have demonstrated mastery of concepts being taught in the classroom, enrichment options are a necessity. These units are designed to help the classroom teacher provide for these needs. They lend themselves easily to a math center arrangement with each student having an individual folder and a check list to record progress. Some of the units can be extensions for units the whole class is studying. For instance, the unit on

DOI: 10.4324/9781003235026-1

coordinate graphing could augment a unit on positive and negative numbers or graphing. The unit on tessellations can be used with a geometry unit, and combinations and permutations can enhance a unit on computation or problem solving.

Providing enrichment options need not be burdensome to the teacher. While the teacher may want to check some of the work himself/herself, it is not necessary for everything to be checked by the teacher as it is completed. Work can be checked by another student or self-corrected. In fact, many of the activities are nearly self-correcting. If the student does the activity correctly, it will look like something, and if it is done incorrectly, it won't look like anything. A quick look will tell you if the student has done the activity correctly. Answers keys can be provided for students who are checking each other's or their own work.

Remember, the emphasis for enrichment units is not, "How many right?" or "How quickly did you finish?" The emphasis should be on promoting thinking, developing perseverance, expanding students' view of mathematics, enjoying a challenge, and on keeping able math students actively involved and enthusiastic about math.

Materials

Line Designs

- pencil
- ruler
- compass
- protractor
- colored pencils
- optional supplies for special projects - cardboard, paint, colored thread, needle, plywood, nails, hammer

Combinations and Permutations

- pencil

Tessellations

- pencil
- ruler
- colored pencils
- pattern blocks
- scissors
- ruler
- tag board

Graphing

- pencil
- ruler
- colored pencils

Independent Study Contract

Name________________________

I began this unit on ________________________________ on ________________________
date

Work Record

Date	I worked on	✓when completed

Conditions of working independently ____

____

____

____

____

____ teacher's signature

____ student's signature

Name________________________

Line designs are patterns that are formed by using only straight line segments to create the illusion of a curve. By connecting points on geometric surfaces (circles, triangles, squares, or intersecting lines) you can create a variety of interesting, attractive designs.

The following illustration shows you the basic steps in making a line design.

1. The basic shape is drawn, in this case a right angle.

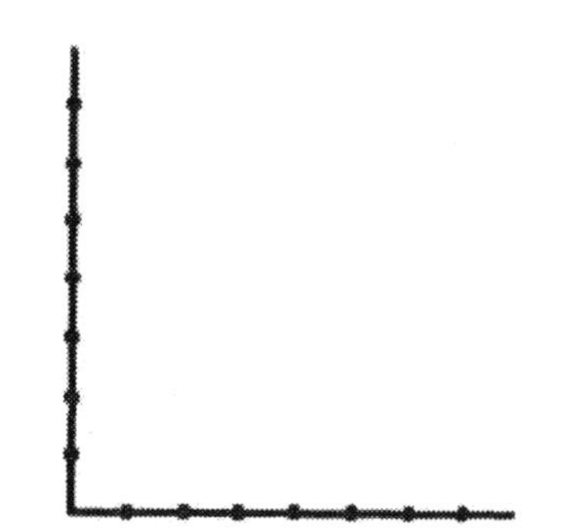

2. Mark the same number of segments on each line.

3. A line is drawn from point A on one line to point A on the other line, and from point B to point B, and so on.

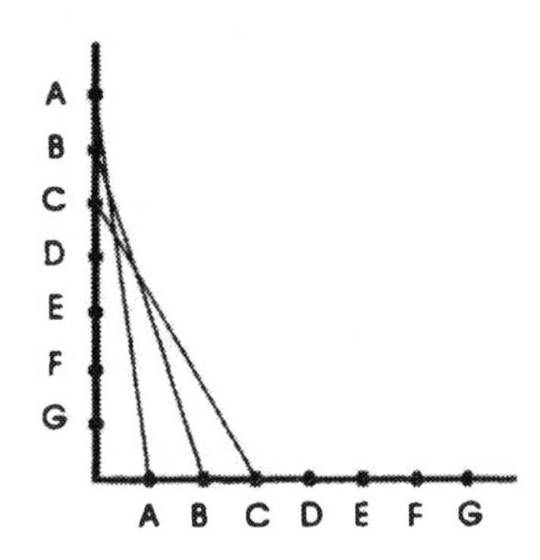

You can change the design by varying:

- the number of points on each side of the design
- the angle that is the basis for the design
- the length of the sides (so that one side is longer than the other).

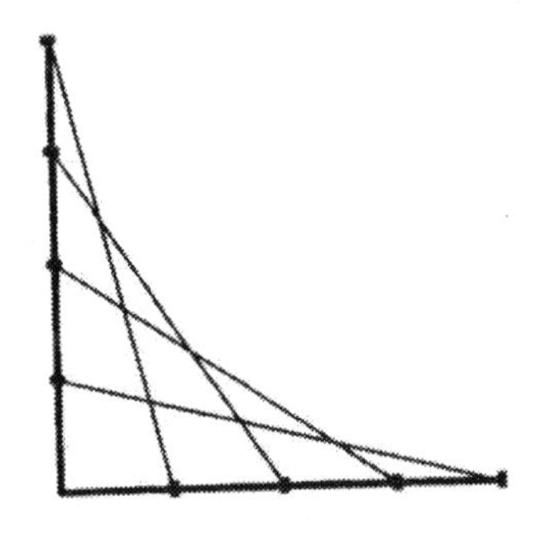

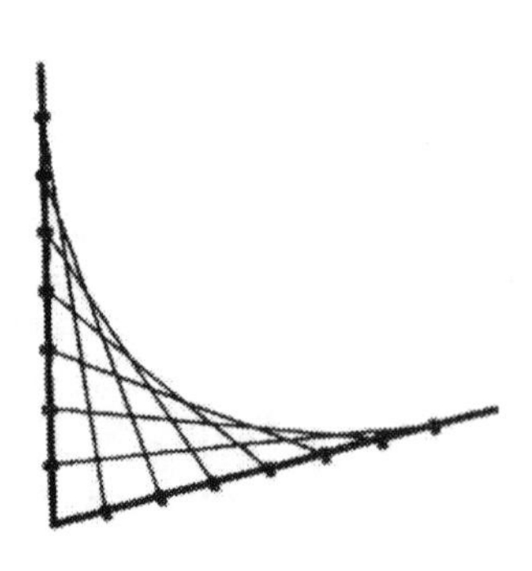

 DOI: 10.4324/9781003235026-3

Name________________________

In this first design you will be drawing lines from point A to point F, from point B to point G, from point C to point H, and so on until your last line is drawn back to point E. The first lines have been drawn for you. Continue drawing lines.

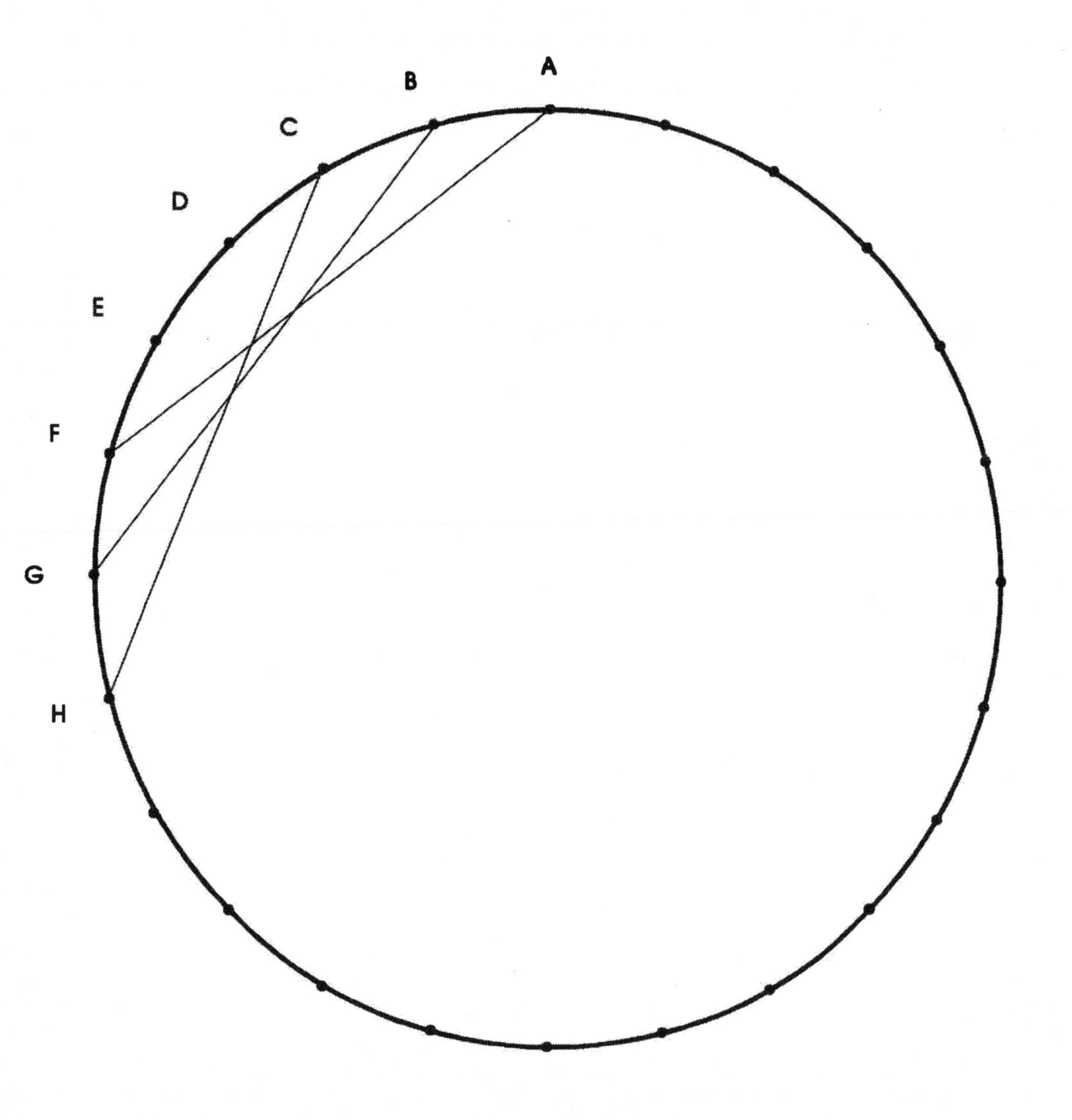

Name________________________

Here are two easy designs that can be created by drawing straight lines to connect the points. Finish each design.

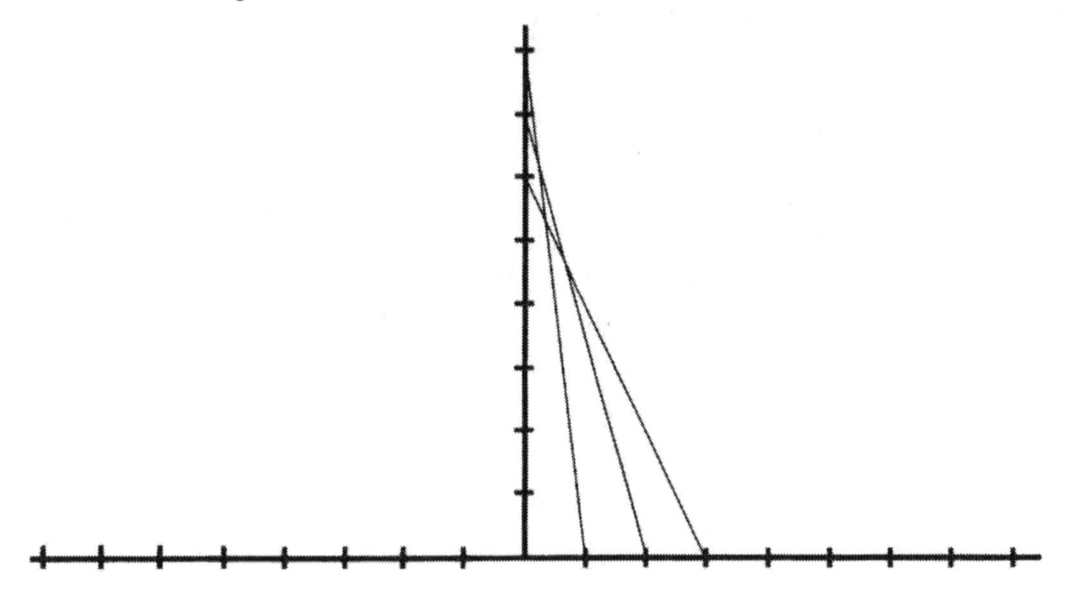

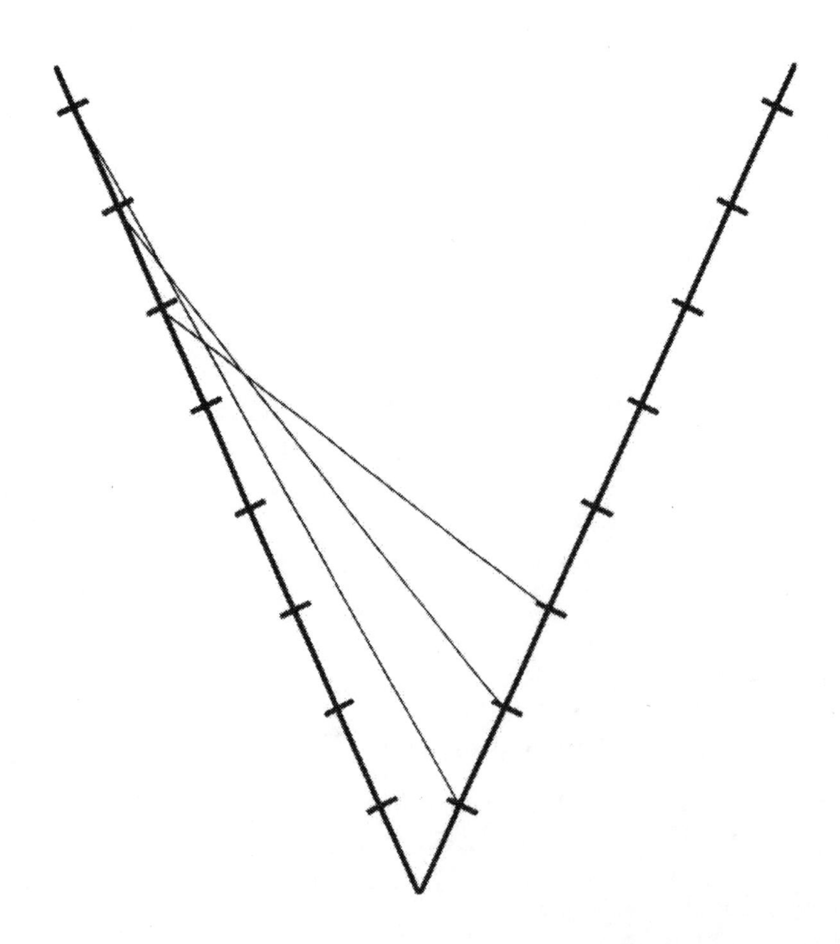

More Angle Designs

Name______________________

Here are more angle designs that can be created by drawing straight lines to connect the points. Finish each design.

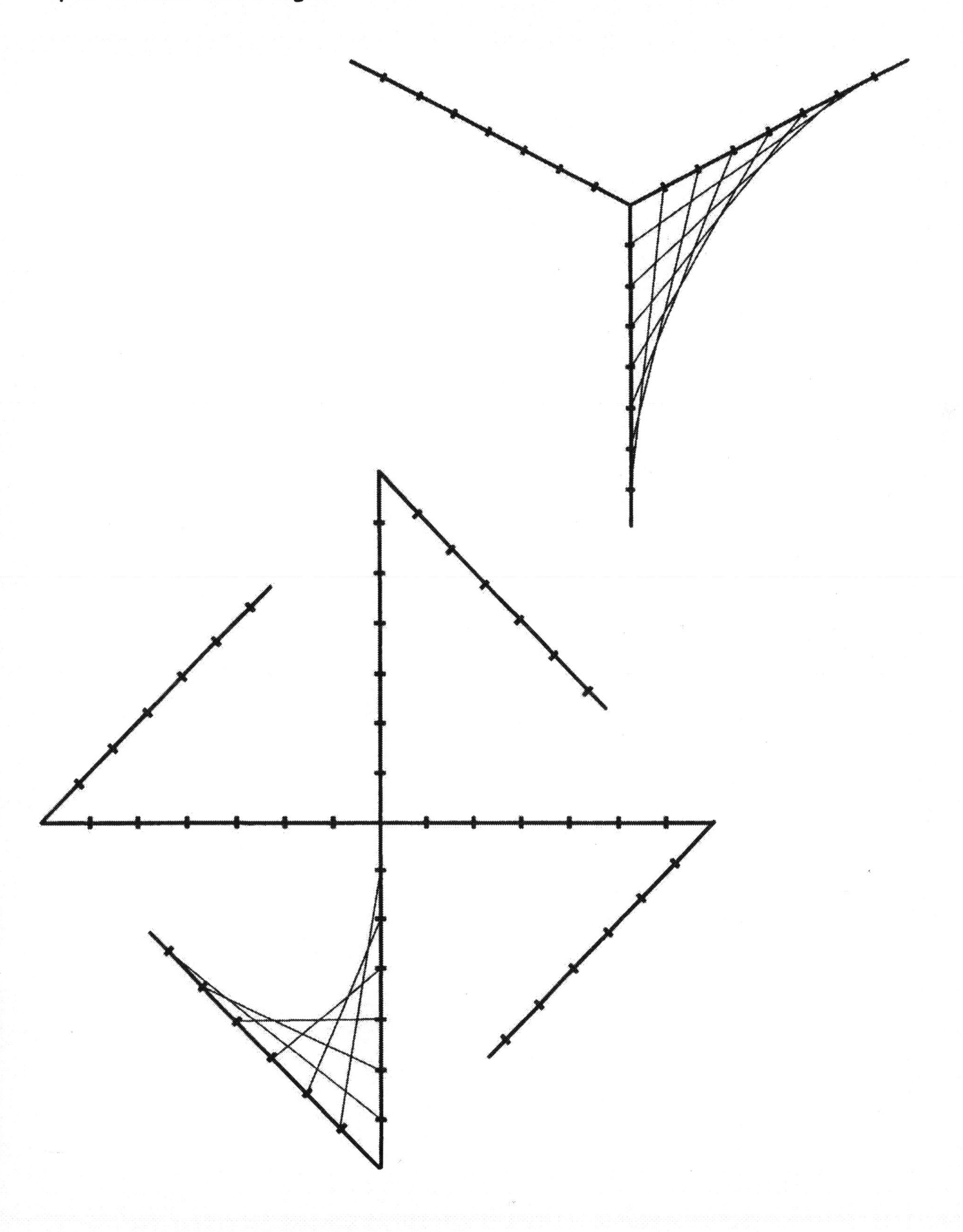

Name______________________

Here are the beginnings of two line designs that can be created by using several angles put together. The first lines have been drawn for you. Continue the pattern.

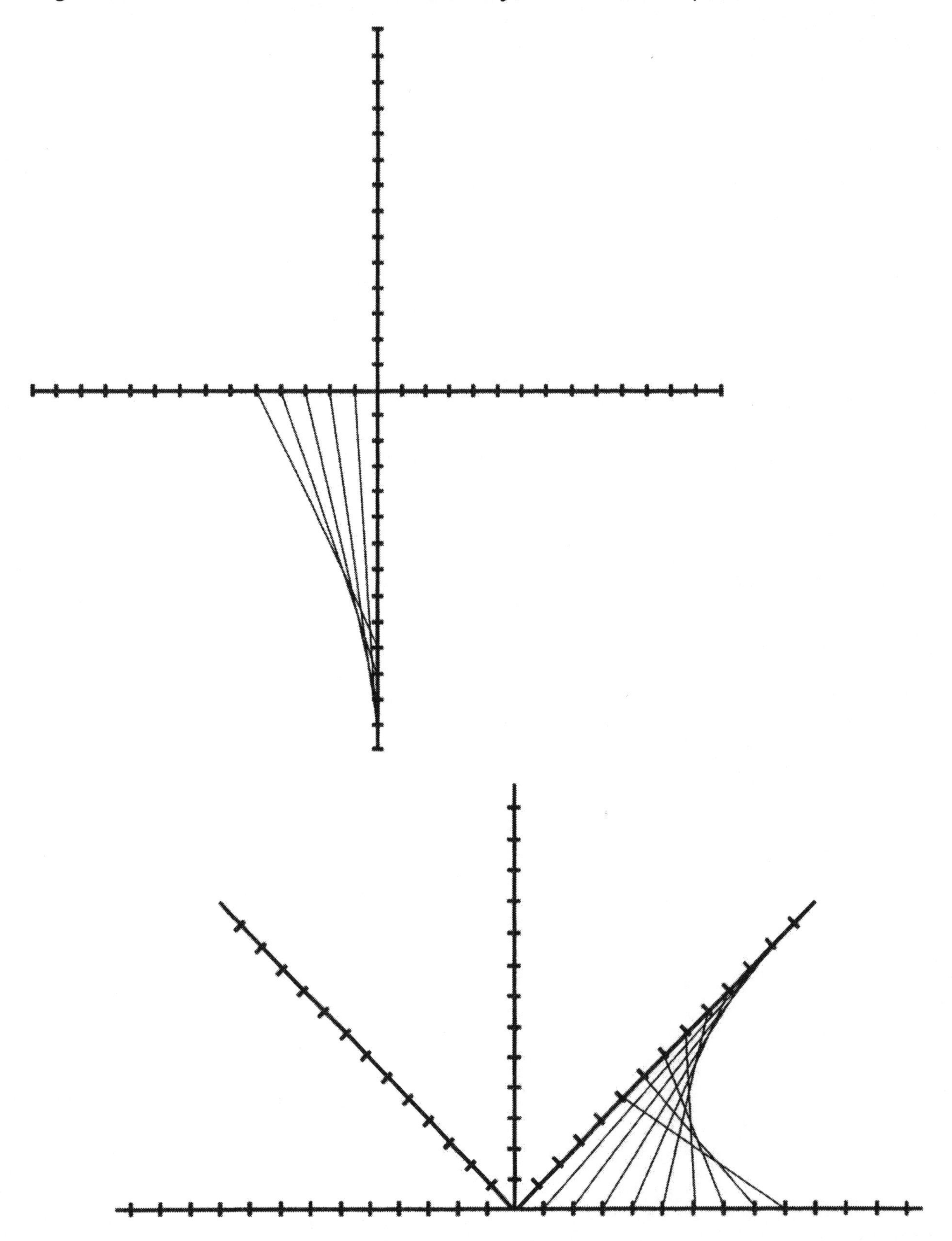

Name________________________

Here is a design that can be made with a square. Continue drawing line segments following the pattern that has been started to make a circular design within the square.

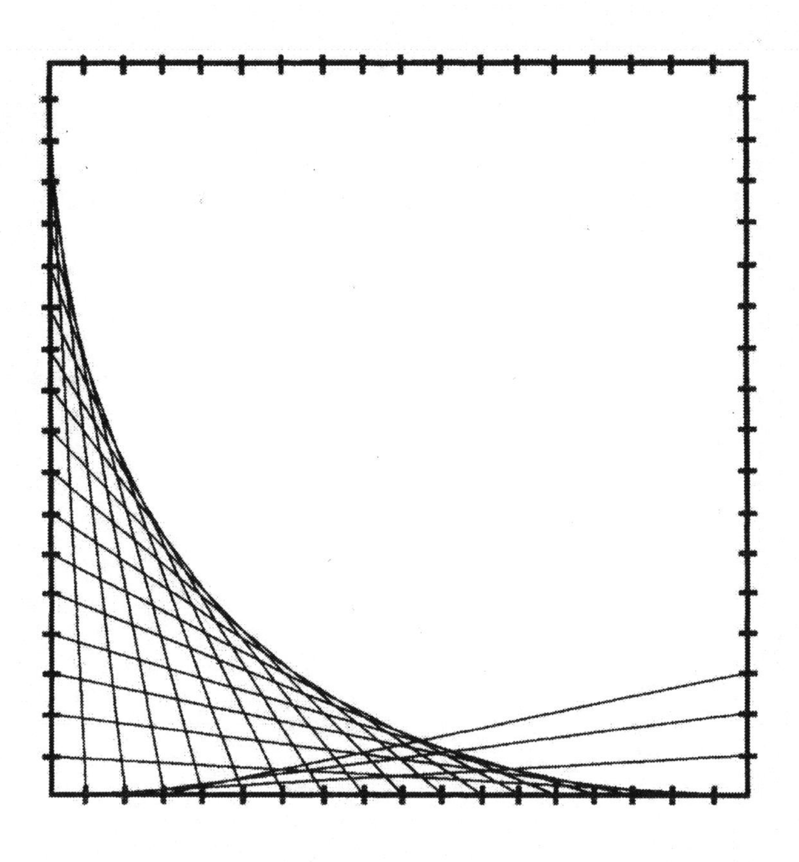

Continue drawing line segments following the pattern that has been started to make a different design within the square.

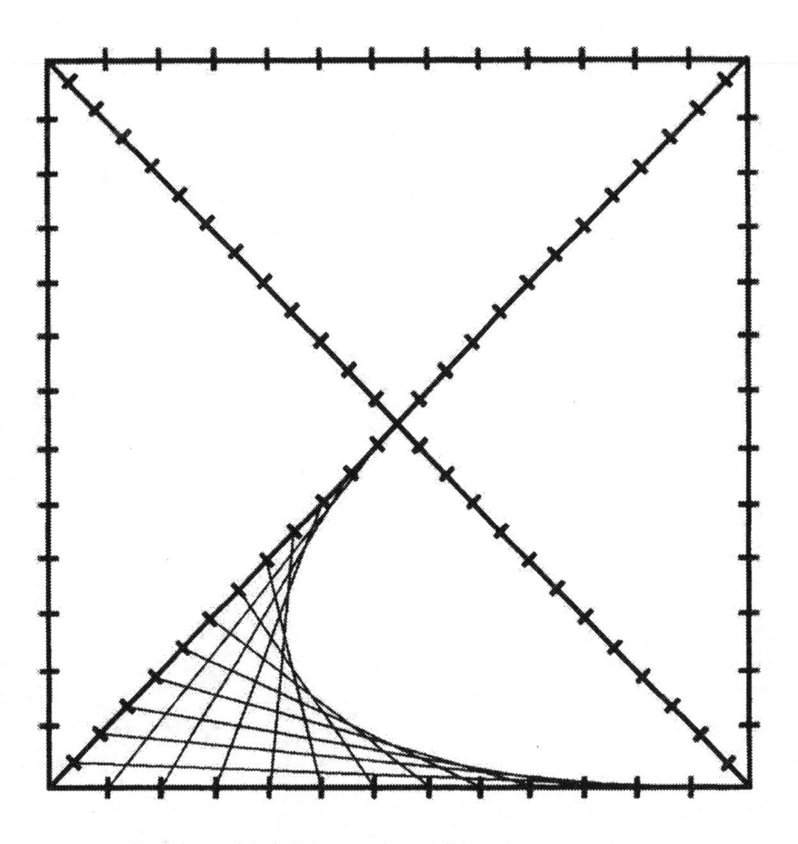

Clover Leaf Design

Name____________________________

Here is a diagram for making a four-leaf clover from a square. One section has been started for you. When you have finished one section, move to the next section and continue connecting points until you have a four-leaf clover shape.

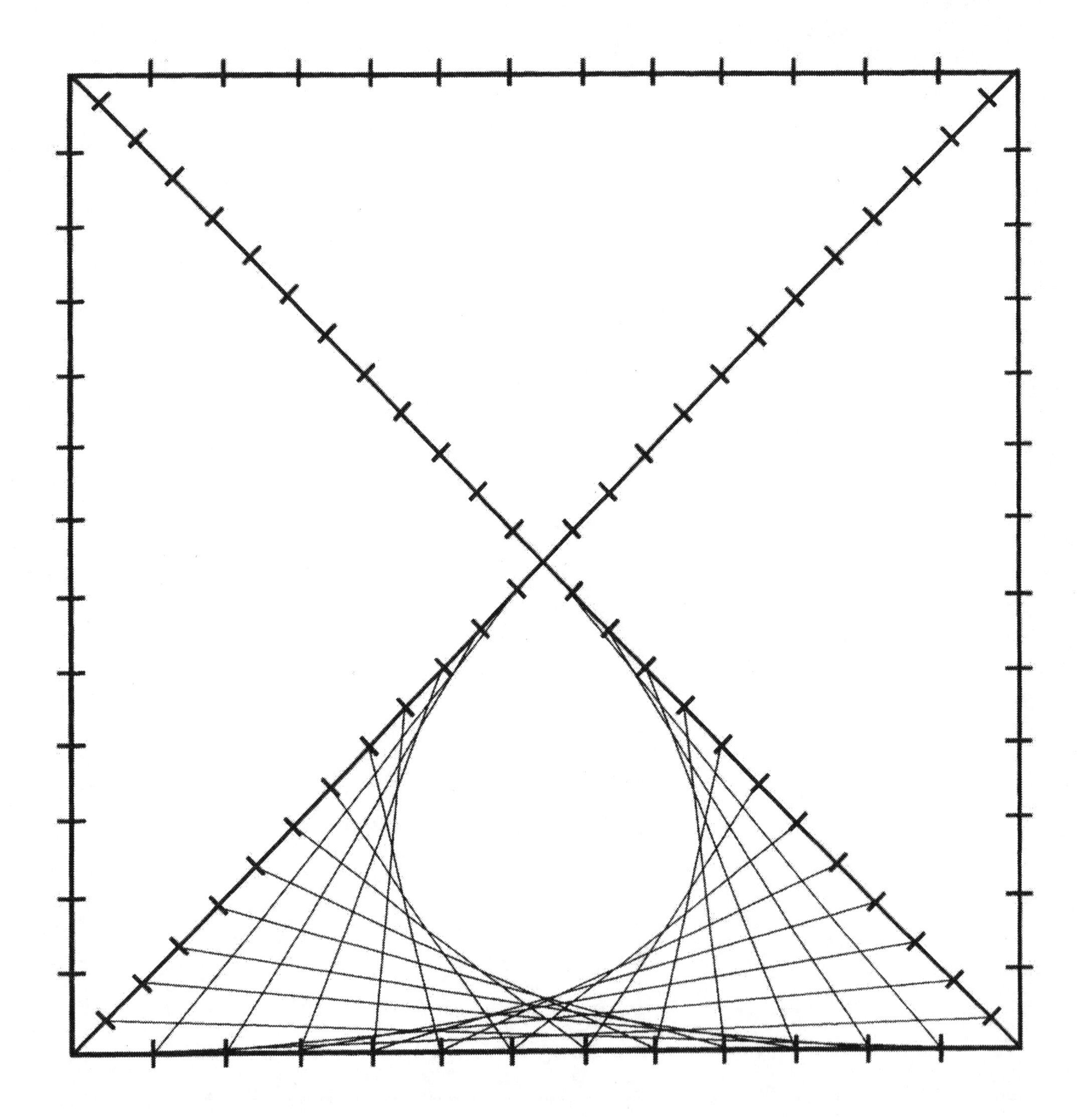

Name ____________________

Here are two triangles that each have the beginning of a line design. Continue the patterns to make two different designs.

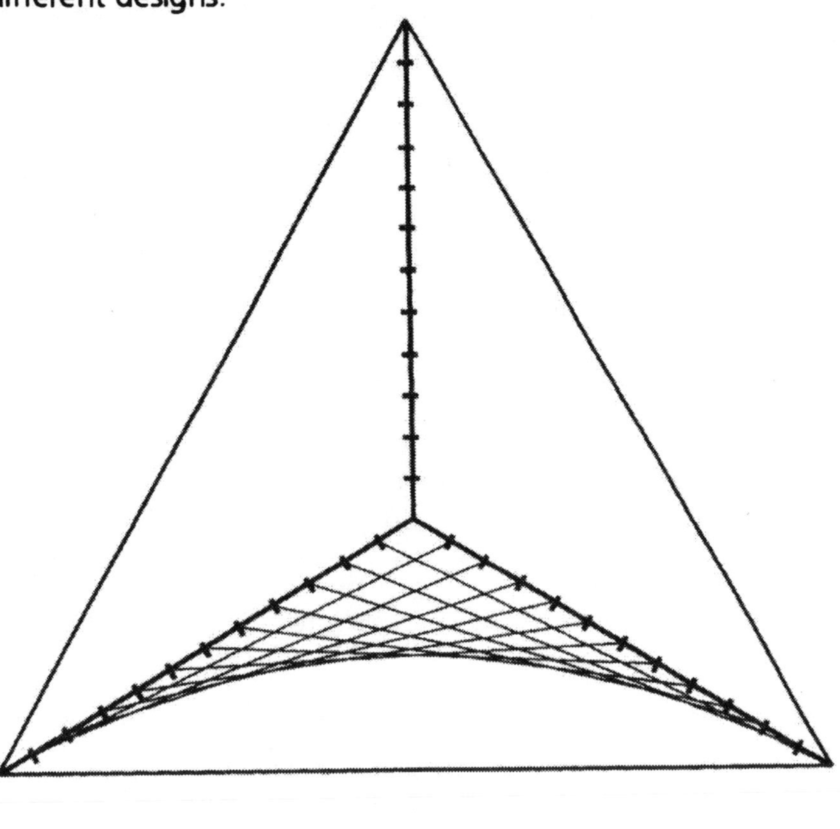

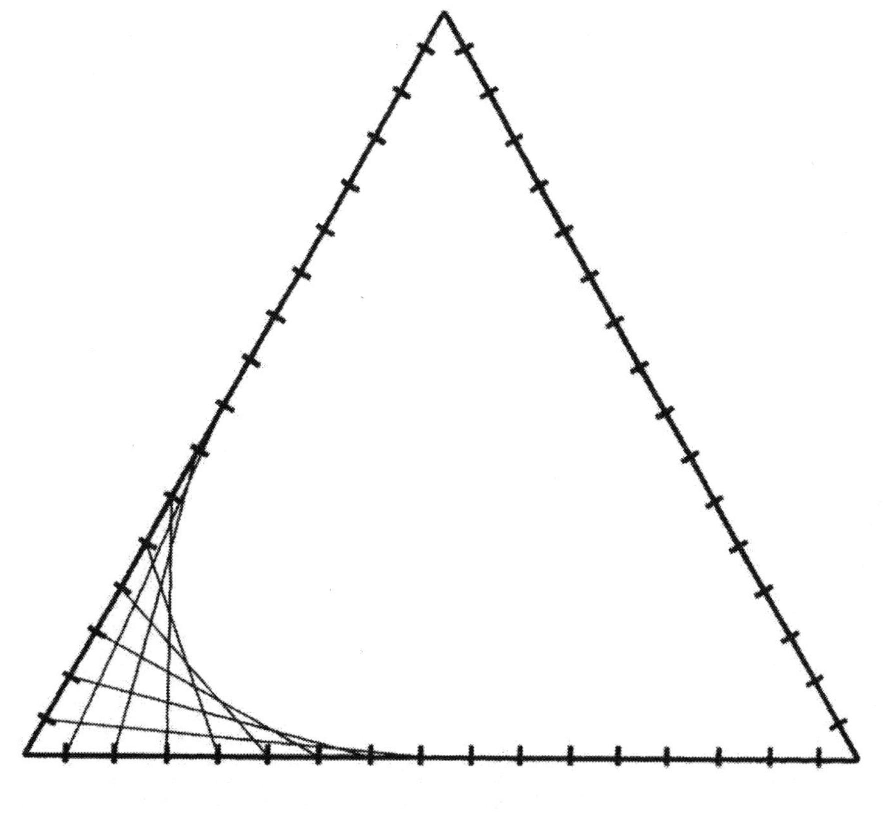

Name____________________

Here are two hexagons that have the beginnings of two different line designs. Continue the pattern.

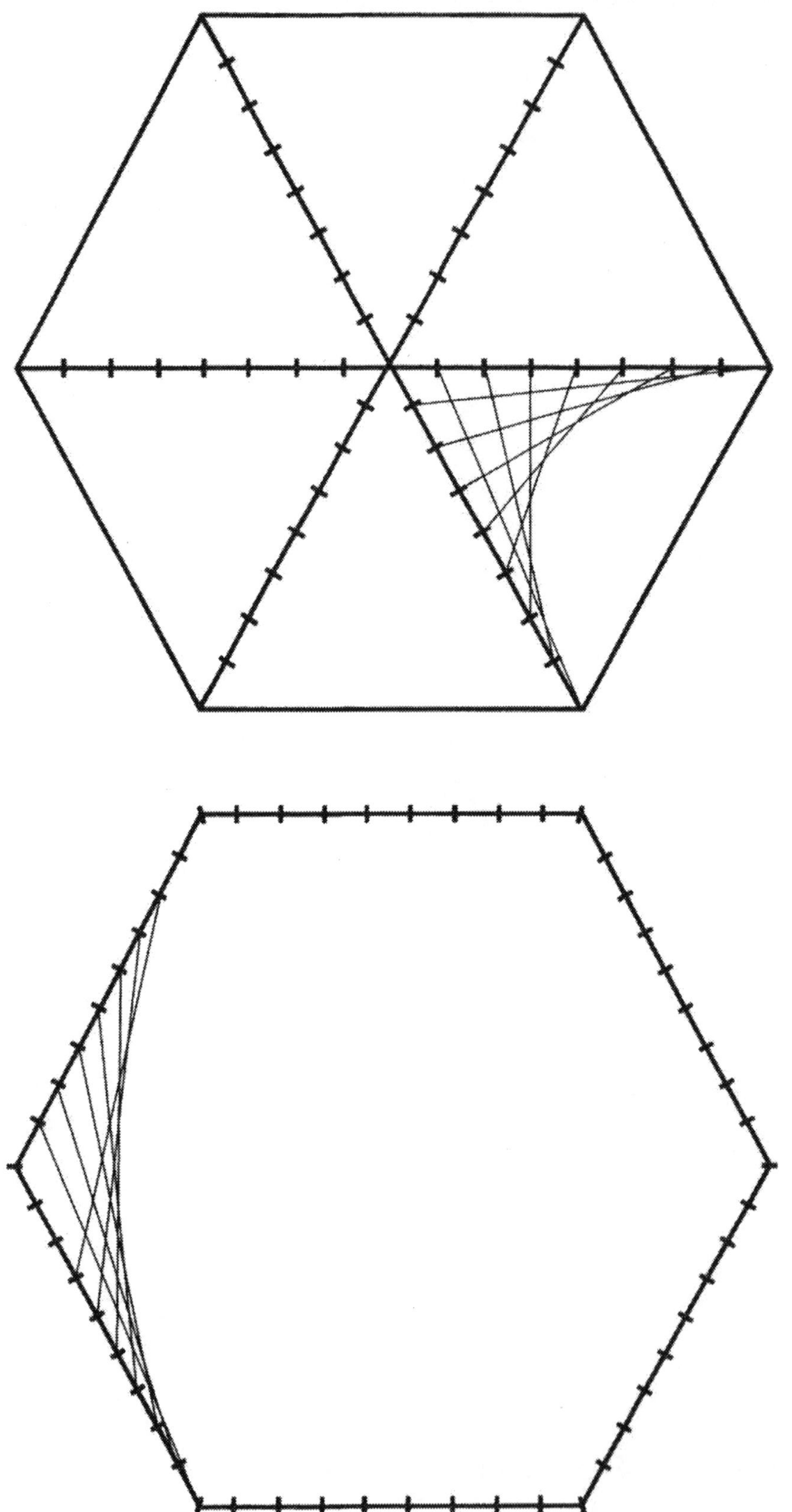

Name ______________________

Sometimes you can combine a couple of line designs to make pictures. Here is a line design that will look like a fish. Continue the patterns for each of the three sections.

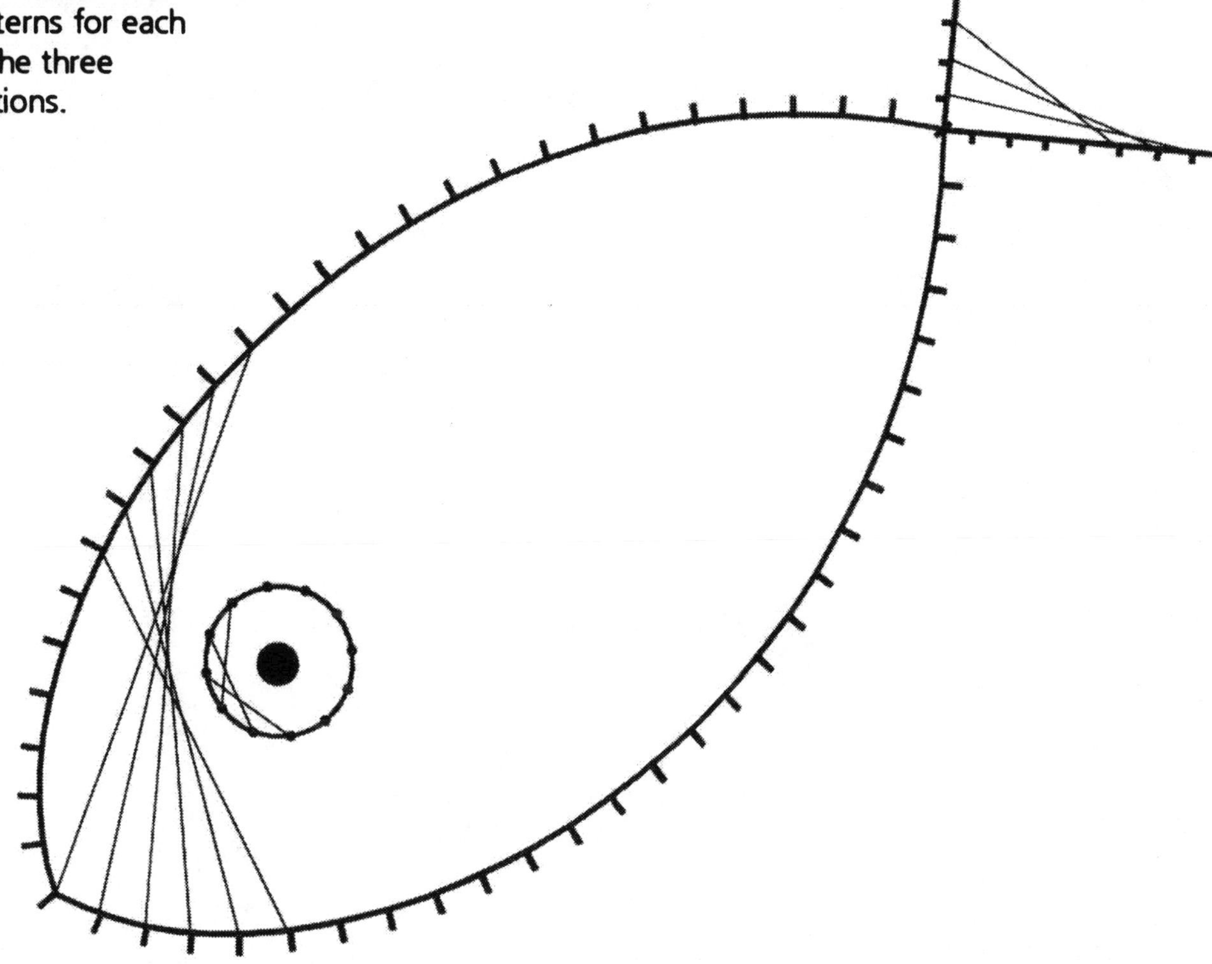

Special Project

Select those shapes that would make the best line drawings and combine several of those shapes into a picture. You may have to add additional lines to make pictures out of the shapes you have chosen.

Design Ideas

Name________________________

Here are several different kinds of line designs. See if you can make some of these designs on another piece of paper.

Name______________________

By using any polygon or angle, you can create your own line design. Follow these directions to create your own special design.

1. Choose a shape.

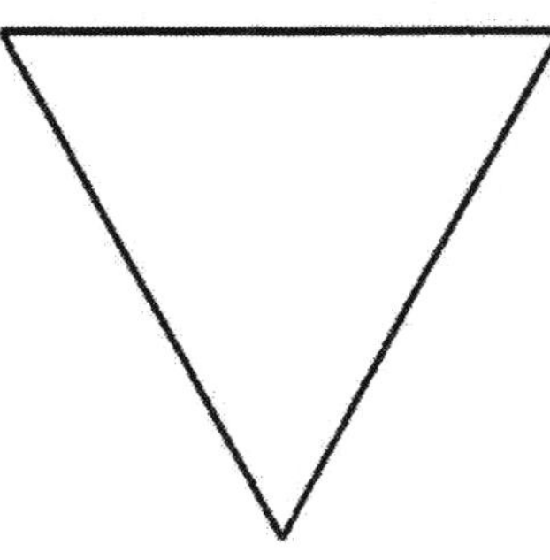

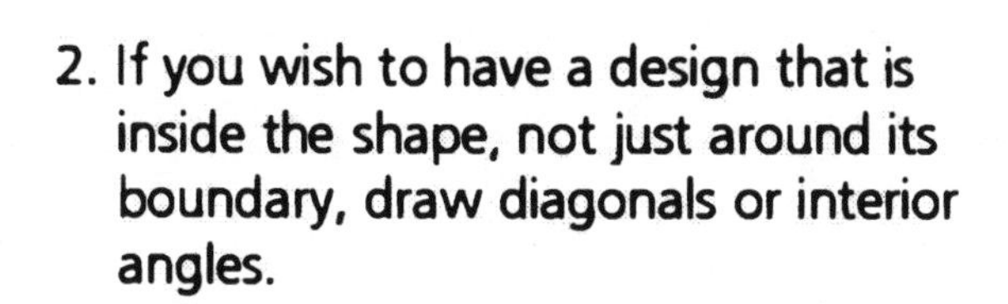

2. If you wish to have a design that is inside the shape, not just around its boundary, draw diagonals or interior angles.

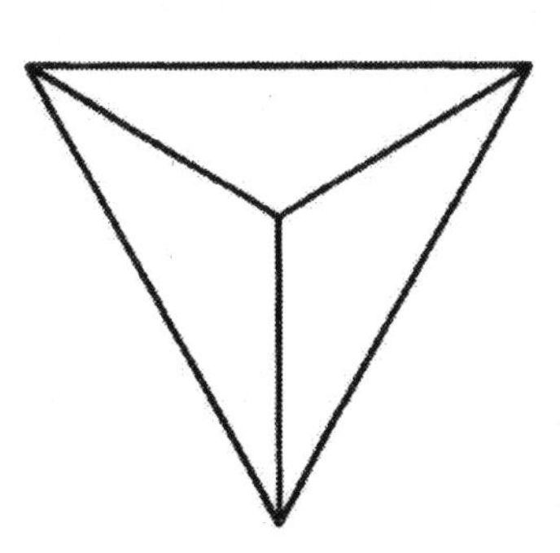

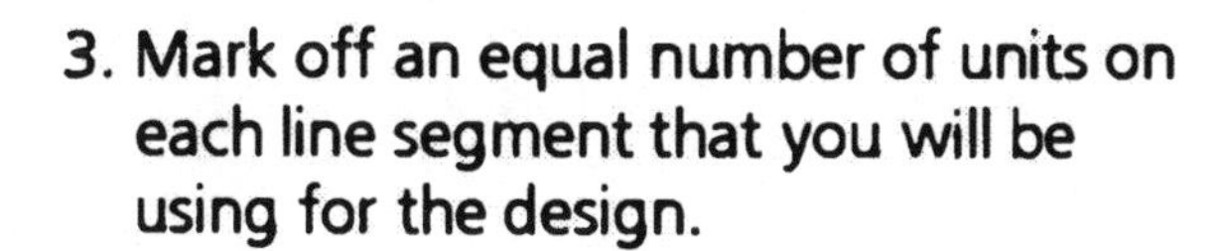

3. Mark off an equal number of units on each line segment that you will be using for the design.

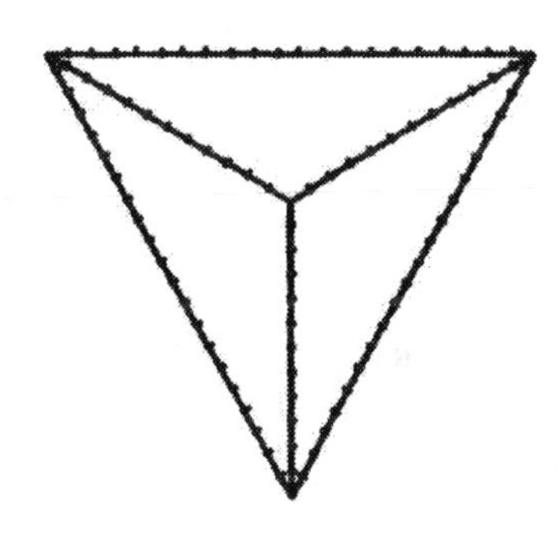

4. Begin with the first section, connecting all points with lines.

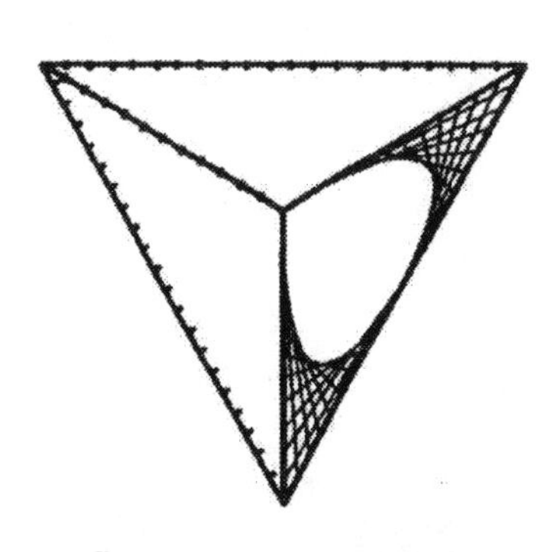

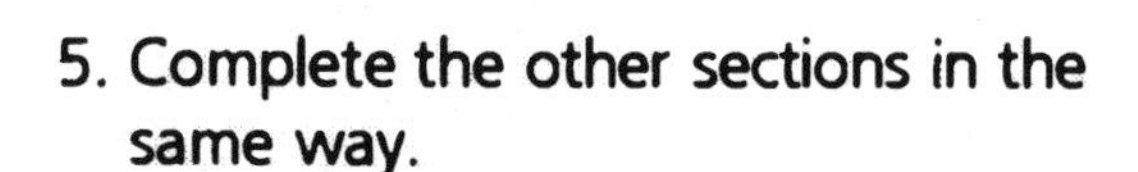

5. Complete the other sections in the same way.

6. Erase unwanted lines.

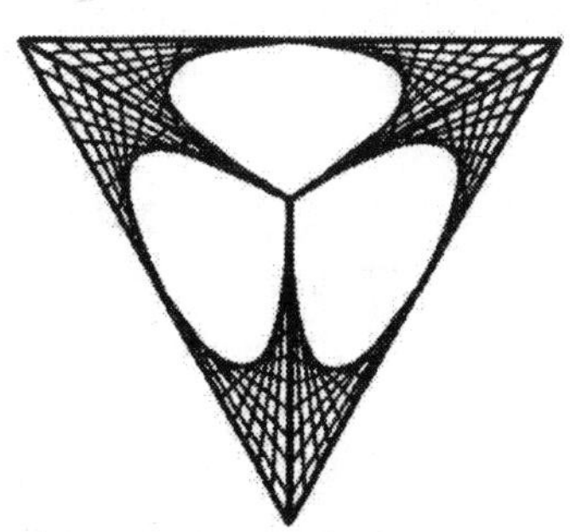

Name______________________

Choose one of these projects.

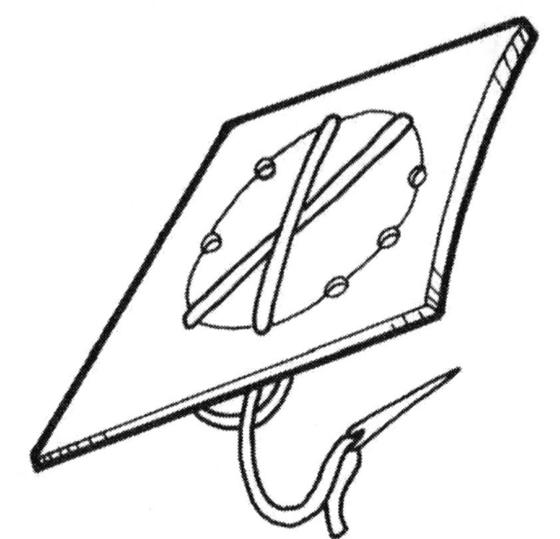

1. **Cardboard and String Design** - Draw your basic shape on a piece of cardboard. Punch a hole through the cardboard for each point on your design. Thread a large needle with thick colored thread. Start at one point and tape one end of the thread to the bottom side of the cardboard. Bring the thread up through the first hole and stretch it fairly tight as you pull it down through a hole to make a straight line with the thread. Continue sewing your design in this fashion until you complete the design. Secure your thread with tape.

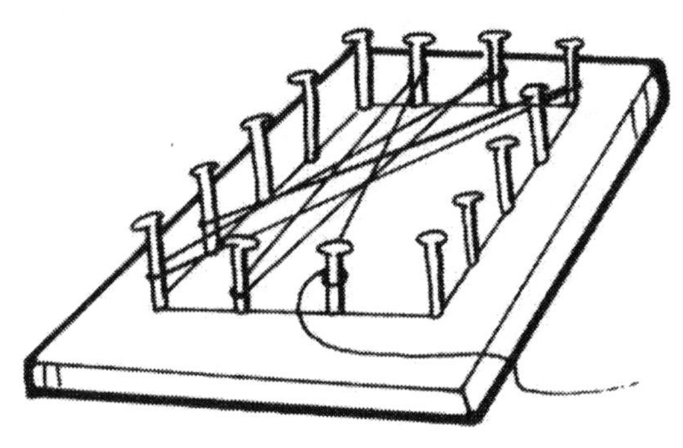

2. **Board Design** - Draw the basic shape on a flat board like plywood. Pound nails where each point on your design should be. Paint the board and let it dry. Tie a piece of colored thread securely around your first nail. Stretch the thread to the n + 1 nail (where n is the interval you have selected). Wrap the thread around that nail, go to the next nail (n + 2), wrap the thread around it and bring it back to the second nail. Continue in this manner until your design is completed. Tie off your thread.

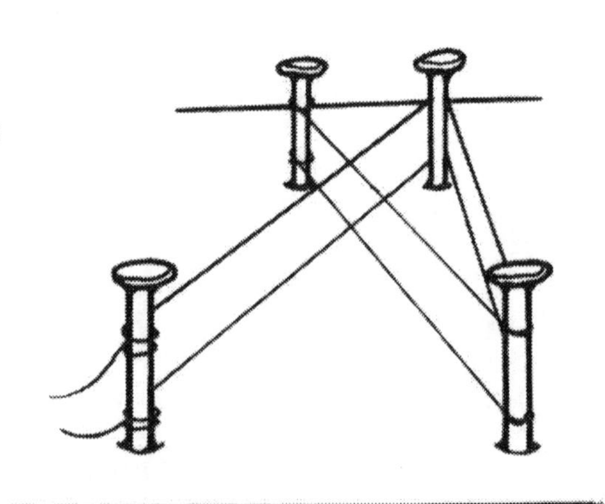

3. **Three Dimensional Board Design** - Prepare a board as in the preceding project, pounding nails in the pattern you have selected. Make your first layer as in the preceding project, using an interval between nails that we will call n. Push this layer down toward the board. Select a different color of thread and make a second layer that has an interval less than interval n. Keep the thread for this layer halfway down the nail. If you wish to do a third layer, you can add another color of thread, wrapped along the top of the nails and with an interval less than the second layer.

Name________________________

In math a **combination** is a way of selecting certain objects from a set of objects. When you select those smaller sets of objects, the order in which they are selected does not matter. For instance, if you had the set of letters (a, b, c) and you wanted to select the letters two at a time, you would have (a, b), (a, c), and (b, c). With combinations, the order of the elements does not matter. The sets (a, b) and (b, a) are considered the same.

Pretend you have three kittens (Fluff, Muff and Pepper) and you want to take pictures of them. You have lots of film, so you want every possible combination of pictures that feature one kitten, two kittens and all three kittens. You would have the following choices:

one kitten	**two kittens**	**three kittens**
Fluff	Fluff and Muff	Fluff, Muff and Pepper
Muff	Fluff and Pepper	
Pepper	Muff and Pepper	

Some times you do not want to consider all the possible combinations, you just want to consider some combinations (like selecting only the pictures of two kittens in the problem above).

1. Four friends (Alan, Burt, Charlie, and Darren) want to ride on the Ferris wheel at the fair. Only two people can ride in a seat. What are all the different ways that the friends could be divided into groups of two?

 DOI: 10.4324/9781003235026-4

Combination Solution Techniques

Name________________________

Two techniques that are helpful in solving combination problems are to **make a drawing** and **make an organized list**. The drawing will often help you visualize the problem that is being presented. The listing lets you systematically keep track of each possible combination. Use these techniques to help you solve these two problems.

1. Jacob has three different ways to go to school (car, walk, bike) and two different ways to go to the mall after school (subway, bus). List the ways Jacob could go from home to school and then to the mall. How many different combinations are possible?

2. What are all the lines that can be drawn connecting these four points? *(Note: $\overline{AB}$ is the same as BA.)*

• A   • B

• D   • C

Name________________________

1. Justin is making a sea life game. He has selected five different kinds of sea life that he will draw on playing tiles so that there are two different animals on each tile. Draw or write the different combinations on the tiles.

2. How many domino pieces are in a double six set? *(Note: Combinations include 0-0, 1-1, 2-2, etc., and a 1-2 piece is the same as a 2-1 piece.)*

Name____________________________

Make a chart to help you find the answers to these problems.

1. Chef Tasty is preparing a menu. He knows that he has only four kinds of fruits (strawberries, bananas, grapes and peaches). How many different kinds of salads can he make if he uses only one fruit in the salad, if he selects two fruits for the salad, if he uses three fruits in the salad, and if he uses all four kinds of fruits?

one fruit	**two fruits**	**three fruits**	**four fruits**
total	total	total	total

2. Brenda is having trouble deciding what to wear to school. She has five different pants and three different sweaters. What are all the possible combinations of outfits she can wear?

Name________________________

1. You and two of your friends put your shoes in a pile and take turns being blindfolded and drawing two shoes out of the pile. What are all the possible combinations you could draw? *(Note: The pair 3 left and 1 right is the same as 1 right and 3 left.)*

2. Jamie has five different pairs of shoes (hiking boots, tennis shoes, black loafers, cowboy boots, and sandals) under his bed (a total of 10 shoes). He reaches blindly under the bed and pulls out two shoes. How many different combinations of shoes are possible? _____ How many of these will result in a matching pair? _______

Name______________________

1. Piper has to take home books for 5 of his classes (English, math, science, geography, and spelling), but he only has room in his backpack for two books. What are the combinations of books that he could put in his backpack?

2. When you go to the showroom to pick out a new car, you find that you have a choice of three colors for the exterior (red, white, yellow) and three colors for the interior (black, tan, blue). How many different combinations of interior and exterior colors do you have to select from?

Name______________________

1. At karate class every class starts with members bowing to each other. If there are six people in the class, how many bows will take place? *(Hint: You do not bow to yourself, and the pair of students A-B is the same as the pair B-A).*

2. A bag has five different-colored marbles (red, blue, green, yellow, and purple). Without looking, you take four marbles out of the bag, note the colors on the listing you have made and put the marbles back in the bag. Show all the different combinations you can get when you take the marbles out of the bag four at a time.

______________________ ______________________

______________________ ______________________

____

Name_______________________

A **permutation** is an arrangement of things in a definite order. Unlike combinations, the order of the items in the subset is what matters with permutations. If you were looking at the different ways you could select two numbers from the set of numbers (1, 2, 3) you would have the following combinations and permutations:

Combinations - (1, 2) (1, 3) and (2, 3)

Permutations - (1, 2) (1, 3) (2, 1) (2, 3) (3, 1) and (3, 2)

In permutations, the set (1, 2) is different from the set (2, 1).

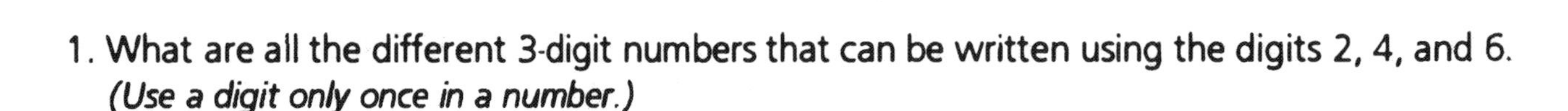

1. What are all the different 3-digit numbers that can be written using the digits 2, 4, and 6. *(Use a digit only once in a number.)*

begins with 2	begins with 4	begins with 6
________	________	________
________	________	________

2. Mrs. Smilovitz is making up a schedule of acts for the talent show. She has three acts, a piano, dance and singing, that she must select for the first three acts to start the show. What are the different ways these acts could be arranged?

piano < sing — dance / dance — sing

dance < piano — sing / sing — piano

sing < ______ ______ / ______ ______

piano - sing - dance

____

____

____

____

____

Permutations of Three Things

Name_______________________

The problems on this page deal with permutations. Remember that in permutations, the order of the subsets is considered.

1. Zoey, Ziggy, and Zac are competing in an art contest. Only one person can get first place, one person second place, and one person third place. What are the different ways that these three people could place in the contest?

(Zoey, Ziggy, Zac)_______________ _______________

_______________ _______________

_______________ _______________

2. You will be using three different kinds of ice cream (vanilla, chocolate, peach) to make double-scoop ice cream cones at your party. You know that everyone will want a different combination of flavors arranged in a certain way, so you are making a chart so your guests can choose which of the three flavors they want and which they want for the bottom scoop and which for the top scoop. They can choose to have both scoops the same flavor.

top scoop
bottom scoop

Name______________________

1. Brendan has assignments in four of his classes (science, math, reading, and spelling), but he only has time to do three assignments, so he is making a list of the different ways he could do three assignments and the order in which he could do the three assignments. Finish the list for him.

(science, math, reading)	______________
(science, reading, math)	______________
______________	______________
______________	______________
______________	______________
______________	______________

Continue your listing on the back of this paper.

2. You and two of your friends are going to a movie. List all the ways the three of you could be seated.

Name______________________

1. Kerry has four frogs that she intends to enter in the Calavaras County Frog Jumping contest. The frog's names are Oink, Bark, Meow, and Twitter. She would be very happy if her frogs could come in first and second places. What are all the possible ways that the frogs could place first or second in the contest?

   The chart shows the possible winners with Oink placing first. Finish this chart and make a similar chart for the other frogs.

1st	2nd	3rd	
Oink	Bark	Meow	Oink - Bark - Meow
		Twitter	Oink - Bark - Twitter
	Meow	Bark	____________
		Twitter	____________
	Twitter	Bark	____________
		Meow	____________

2. Hilarie has three different bears (named Alberto, Burt, and Chacha) that she lines up on her bed. She changes the arrangement every day. What are all the different arrangements she can make with the three bears?

Name____________________

1. ***Four candidates are running for class president. How many different ways can the candidates' names be listed on the ballot?*** ______

One way to solve this problem is to make a chart showing the different arrangements of the candidates (call them candidates A, B, C, and D). The chart would look like this:

1st	2nd	3rd	4th
A	B	C	D
A	B	D	C
A	C	B	D
A	C	D	C
A	D	C	B
A	D	B	C

There are six different arrangements with candidate A's name first. There will also be six arrangements with B first, six with C first and six with D first, giving a total of 6 + 6 + 6 + 6 or ______ arrangements.

If you didn't want to list all the possible arrangements, another way to solve this problem is to think of how many different ways you can fill each slot on the ballot.

4			

There are 4 choices for the first slot.

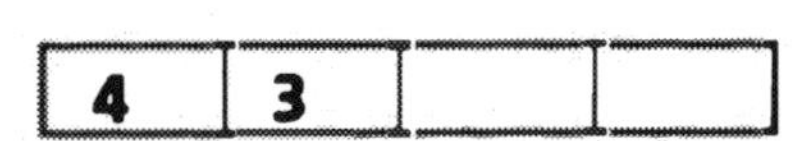

Once that slot has been filled, there are 3 choices for the second slot.

4	**3**	**2**	**1**

Once the people have been chosen for the first and second slots, there are 2 choice for the third slot and 1 for the fourth slot.

4 x 3 x 2 x 1 = 24

When these numbers are multiplied, it gives us the number of possible arrangements (permutations).

2. Use the multiplication technique to solve this problem:
Five runners enter a race. How many different first, second, and third place finishes can occur?

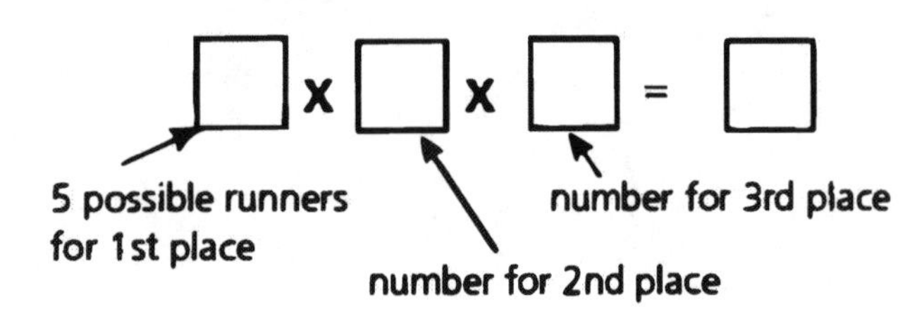

Name________________________

1. Mrs. O'Brien gave each group of students six cards with numerals on them. She told the groups to place the cards face down, select four cards randomly and arrange them to make the largest number. How many different number arrangements are possible for the four cards?

2. Bernie is arranging his collection of model cars on a shelf. He finds that he only has room for three of his six models. He six cars are a Mustang, Corvette, Jaguar, Lamborghini, Model A, and Porsche. How many different ways can he arrange three of his six cars?

Permutation Practice 1

Name________________________

1. You lost your friend's phone number, but you remember that the first three numbers are 544 and the last four numbers include the digits 2, 7, 3, and 9. How many different phone numbers are possible from the different arrangements of these four digits?

2. Six horses are in a race. In how many different ways can the horses place first, second, and third?

Name______________________

1. The courthouse flies the city, state and country flags. How many different ways can the three flags be arranged on the flag pole?

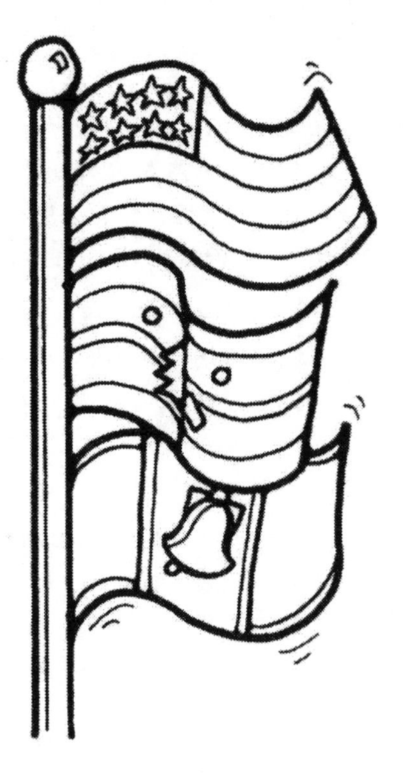

2. Four cheerleaders are having their picture taken for the school annual. How many different ways can they be arranged?

Name________________________

A **tessellation** is an arrangement of congruent shapes on a flat surface. This ancient form of decoration dates back to the 4th century B.C. These geometric patterns are made of one or more shapes that are fit together to make a repeating pattern – a tessellation. A design pattern is a tessellation if:

- it is made of one or more congruent shapes that can be extended in every direction to cover a surface
- the pattern pieces fit together without any gaps or overlapping.

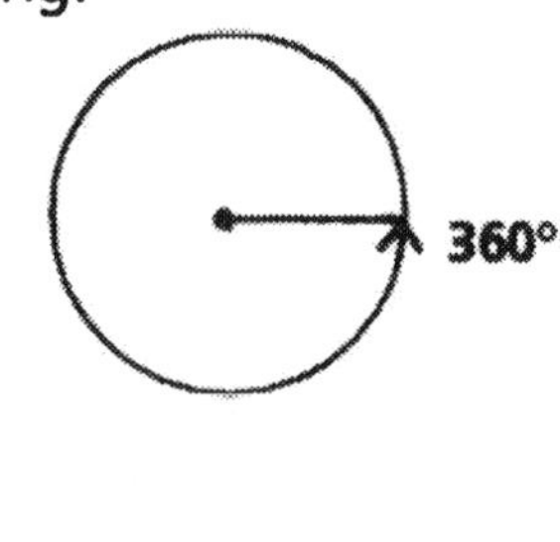

There are only three regular polygons that will always form a tessellation using only one shape – a **square,** an **equilateral triangle**, and a **regular hexagon**. This is because of the relationship between their interior angles and the measure of a complete rotation around a vertex (point). The number of degrees in a complete rotation around the vertex is 360°.

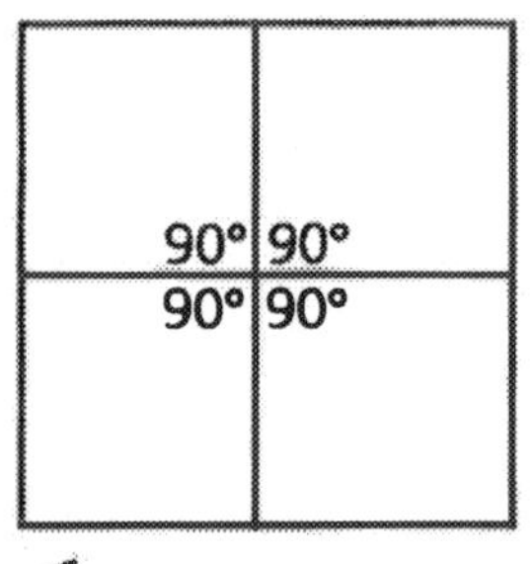

An **equilateral triangle** has three 60° angles. Six triangles would be needed to make a complete rotation of 360° around a vertex. A **square** has four 90° angles. It takes four squares to make a complete rotation around the vertex. The angles of a **regular hexagon** are 120°. Three hexagons will fit together to make a complete rotation around the vertex.

The figure above shows how four squares can tessellate around a point. In the space below are two vertices. Cut out the triangle and hexagon on the right. Trace six triangles around one of the points and three hexagons around the other point to show how these two polygons can tessellate.

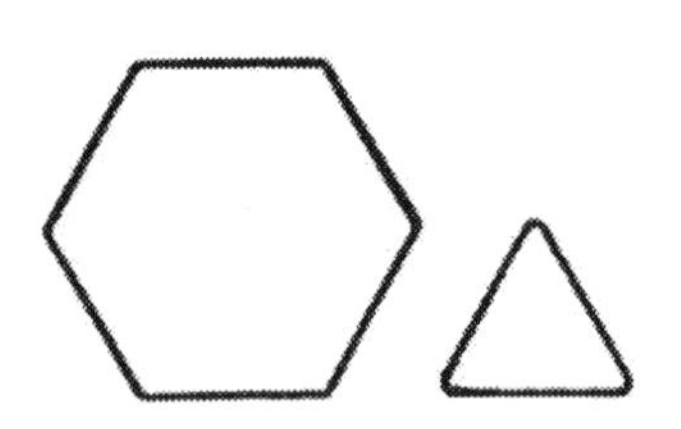

•   •

DOI: 10.4324/9781003235026-5

Name________________________

Squares are one of the three regular polygons that will always tessellate using only one shape. This is because each angle is 90° and four of these angles will form a rotation of 360°. Other four-sided figures will also make tessellations.

All rectangles have four ______ ° angles. Therefore, all rectangles will also tessellate. With rectangles, however, you can get a greater variety of patterns than you can with squares. You can rotate (turn) and translate (slide) the basic shape to form interesting repeating patterns. You can also combine rectangular and square shapes to make tessellating patterns.

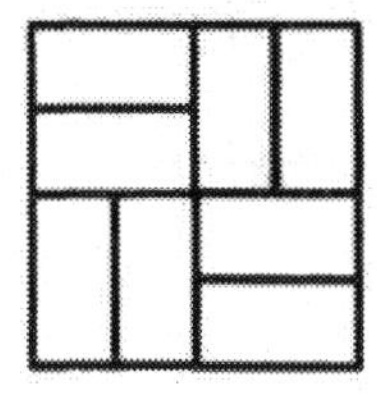

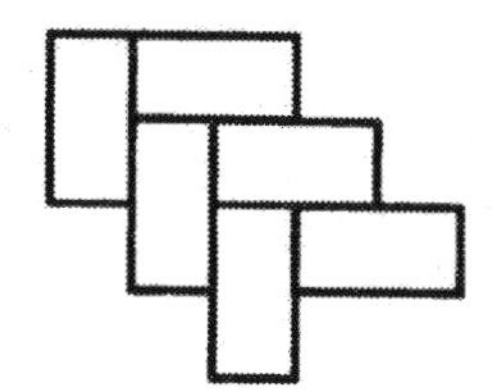

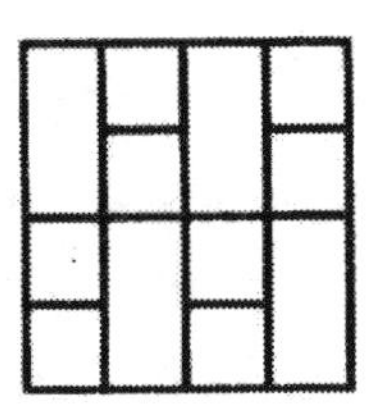

On the grid draw and color a tessellating design using one or more of these shapes. Continue the pattern to the edge of the grid.

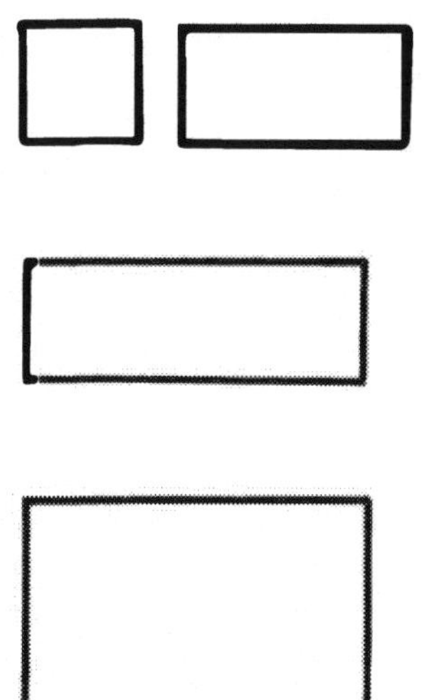

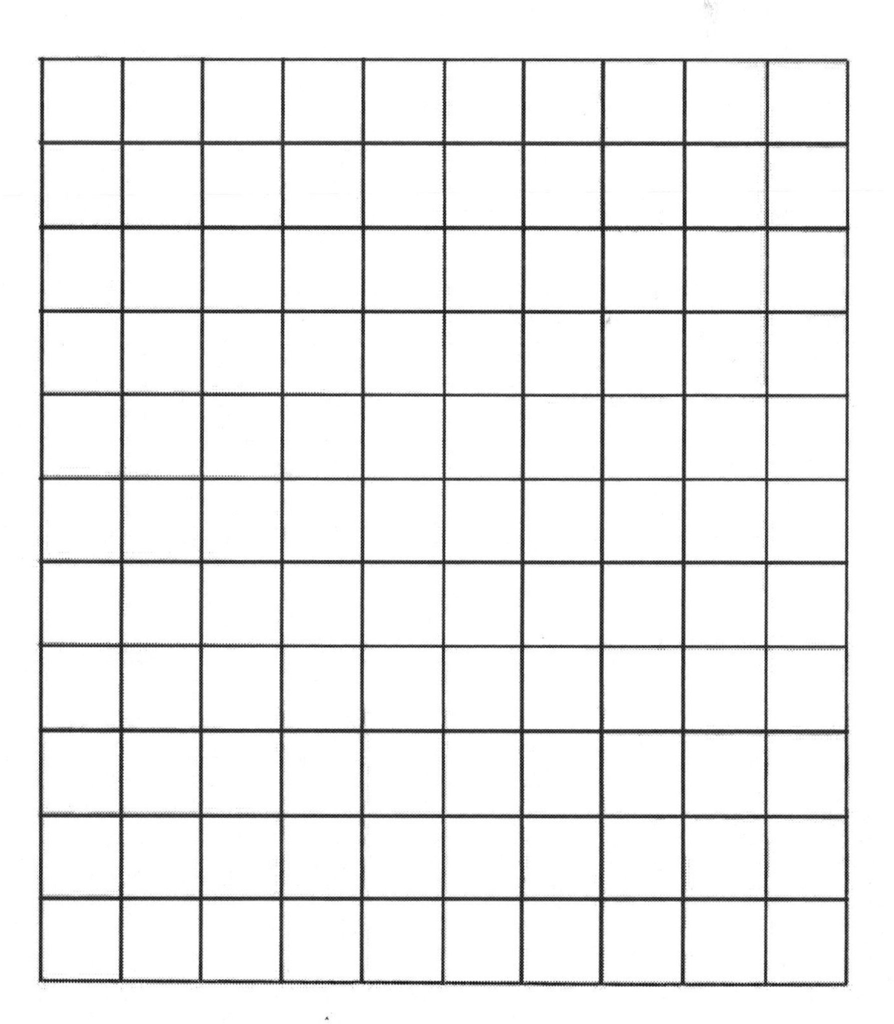

Name________________________

We know that an equilateral triangle will tessellate. We also know that the sum of the angles of any triangle is 180°. It would seem, then, that all triangles will tessellate, though the pattern will not be as regular as with an equilateral triangle. Here is a project that will demonstrate that any triangle will tessellate.

1. Cut any triangle from a piece of cardboard or poster board.
2. Use this shape as a pattern and carefully trace it 18 times on a piece of construction paper.
3. Cut out the 18 triangular shapes.
4. Arrange and glue the construction paper triangles in the space below to form a tessellation. There should be no gaps or overlapping where the triangles meet each other, though you may have empty spaces at the edge of the design where the triangles do not completely meet the edge of the paper.

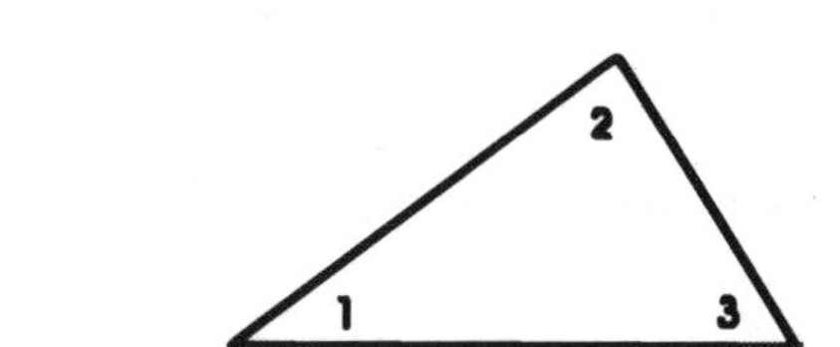

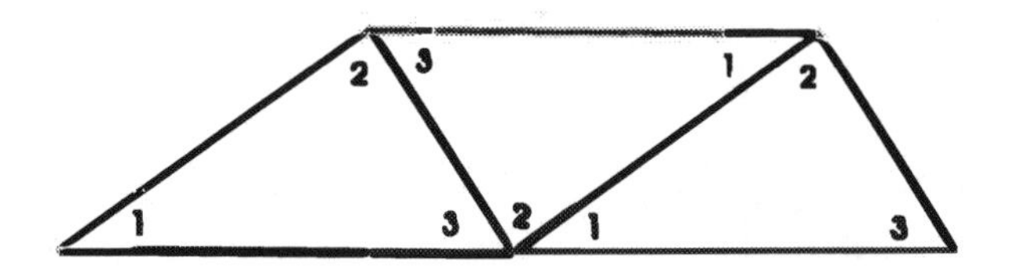

Quadrilateral Experiment

Name_______________________

Along the sides of this page are 12 congruent triangles. Follow these instructions to discover if quadrilaterals made from congruent triangles will tessellate.

1. Color six of the triangles red.
2. Cut out all 12 triangles.
3. Using one red and one white triangle for each new polygon, make 6 different shapes with congruent sides adjacent to each other (as shown below).
4. Glue your triangles on the space below to show 6 different shapes. Two are outlined for you. You should be able to form 6 different polygons, each one made of two triangular shapes.

Choose one of these shapes and use it to make a tessellation on a separate piece of grid paper.

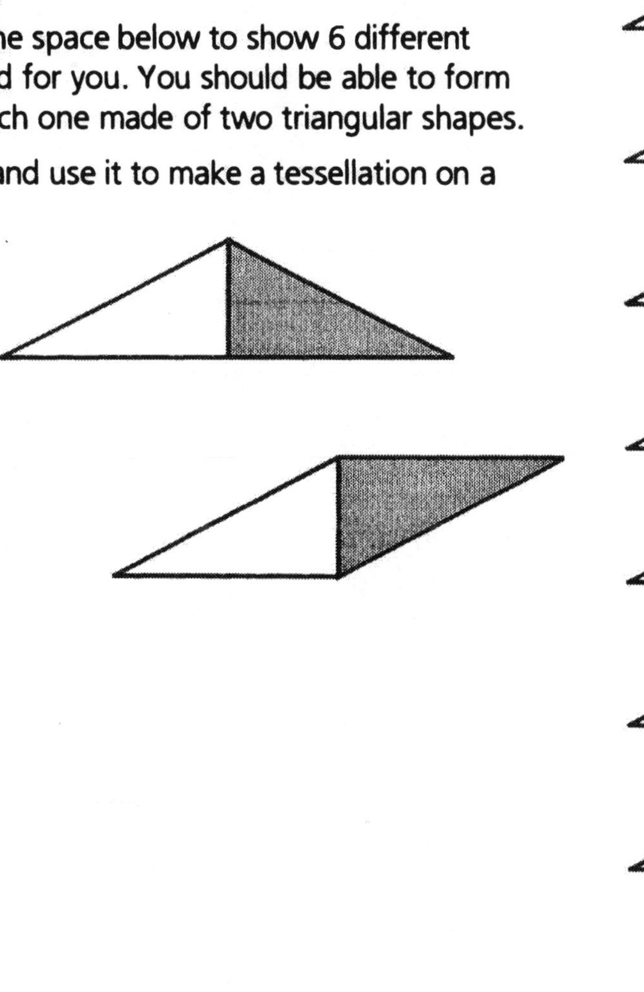

Quadrilateral Experiment

Name________________________

While there are only three regular polygons that form tessellations containing only one shape, many irregular shapes will also tessellate. Try this experiment to discover if all quadrilaterals will tessellate.

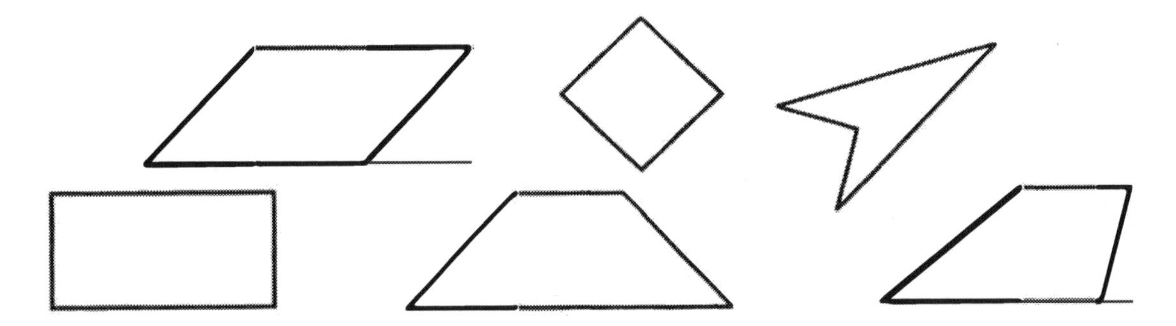

Using a ruler, draw a line connecting two opposite vertices of each quadrilateral above.

What do you find? ____

Quadrilaterals can be divided into two triangles. All triangles tessellate, because the sum of the angles is 180° and six congruent triangles can be placed so that they will form 360° around a vertex.

Here is a grid of triangles (a triangular tessellation). Color in a shape that is made of two triangles. This will be your tessellating shape. Using a colored pencil or dark pen, extend a pattern using this shape.

Name________________________

Semi-regular tessellations are combinations of two or more regular polygons (all sides equal and all angles equal). The edges of the polygons that are used must be equal and the combinations of polygons at every vertex must be the same. Here are two examples of semi-regular tessellations.

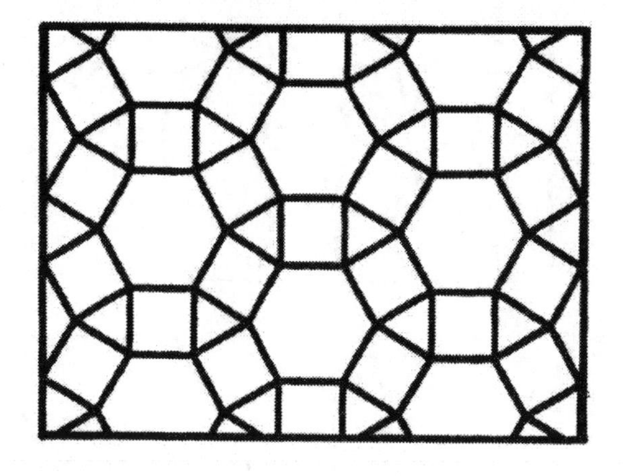

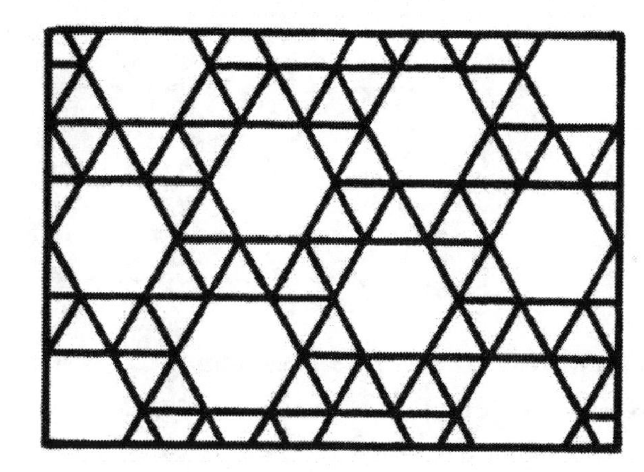

Get yellow, green and orange pattern blocks or cut out several copies of the shapes on the right. Use the shapes to create a mosaic-type design in the space below. There should not be any gaps between your pattern blocks.

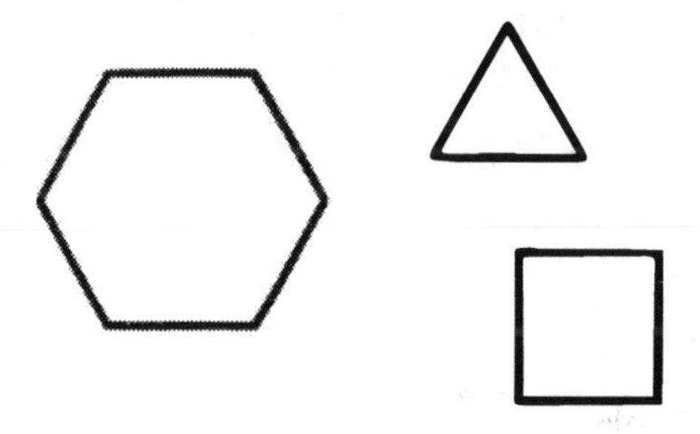

Name________________________

Tessellating designs have been used in art for centuries. Our word *tessellate* comes from the Latin word "tessella." Tessella were the small square stones used in Roman mosaics. Early artisans used tessellations on floors, walls and ceilings.

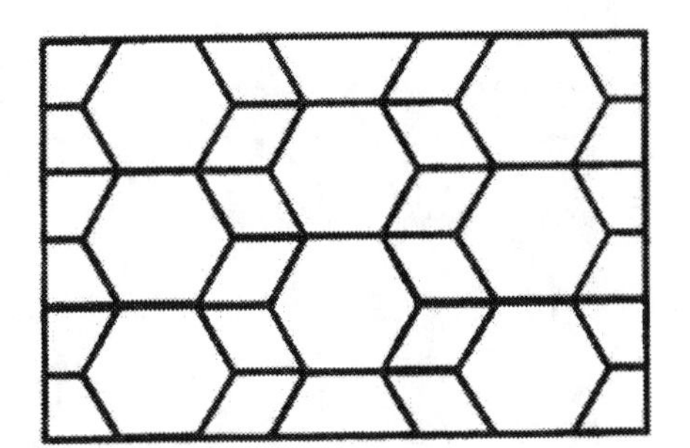

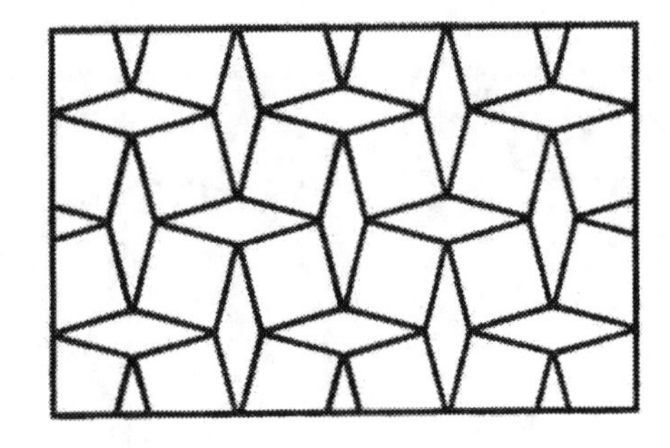

An easy way to create a tessellating pattern is to use pattern blocks. Choose two or three different pattern block shapes or cut out the shapes on the right and make 10 copies of each shape. Arrange the pieces to create a mosaic-type design in the space below. There should be no gaps between your pattern pieces.

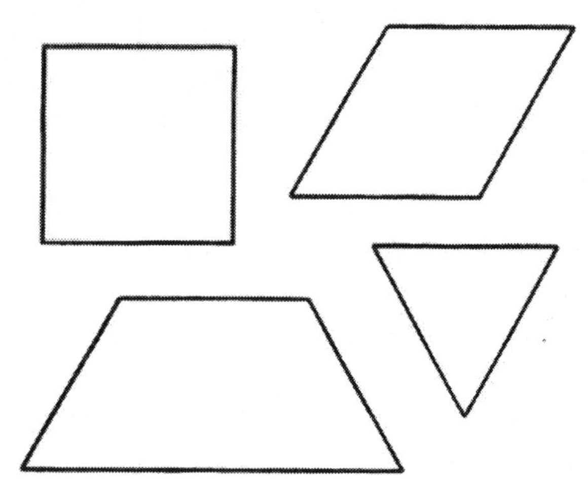

Name________________________

One easy way to create your own tessellating design is to draw parallel lines on a grid. Follow these instructions to make your own design on the grid below.

1. Decide on a zigzag pattern, like *up two and over two, down two and over two.*

2. Draw a line on the grid that follows that pattern.

3. Move down several spaces on the grid and draw line segments that are parallel to the original lines you drew. Continue drawing parallel lines.

4. To make a tessellating quadrilateral, draw vertical lines to connect the points where the lines changed direction. To make a tessellating hexagon draw vertical lines only at every other turning point.

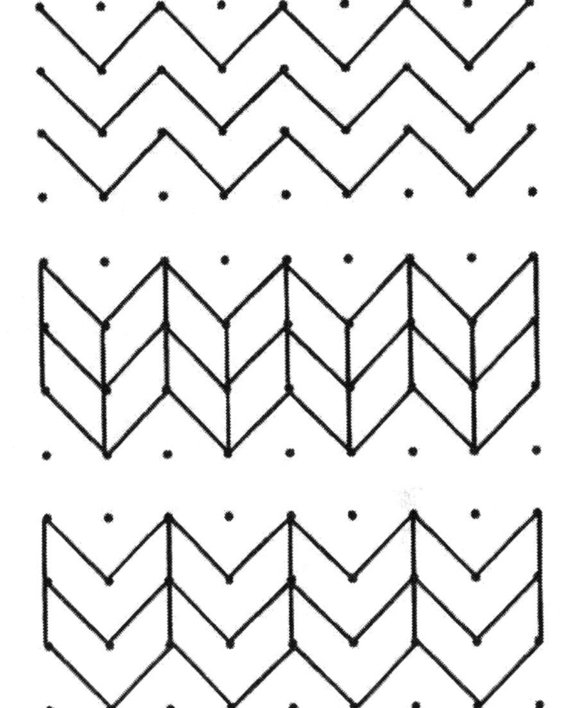

Create your own tessellation in the space below using the parallel line technique.

Tessellations on Dot Paper

Name________________________

Tessellations can be created by drawing designs on dot paper. You can choose to draw one shape or can combine several compatible shapes. The design you choose must be able to extend in every direction. Here are some examples.

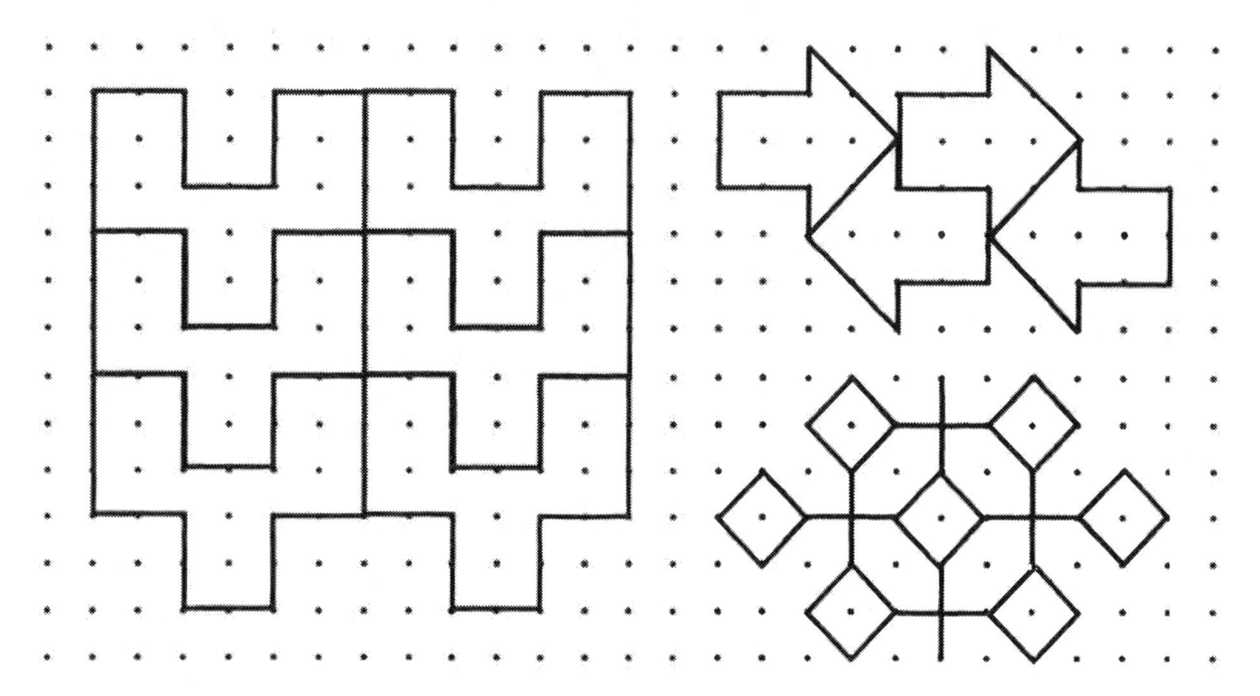

Use the dot grid below to make your own tessellating design. Choose a shape that is simple and that is able to fit with itself or with a complementary shape. Begin at one edge and draw the shape or shapes to fill the dot grid.

Name________________________

Another easy way to make tessellations is by drawing a simple shape and then moving the shape over and redrawing it in a new position. Here are two examples of designs that have been created by drawing a pattern using one shape and then offsetting the pattern and redrawing it. This technique will create new shapes that form a tessellating design.

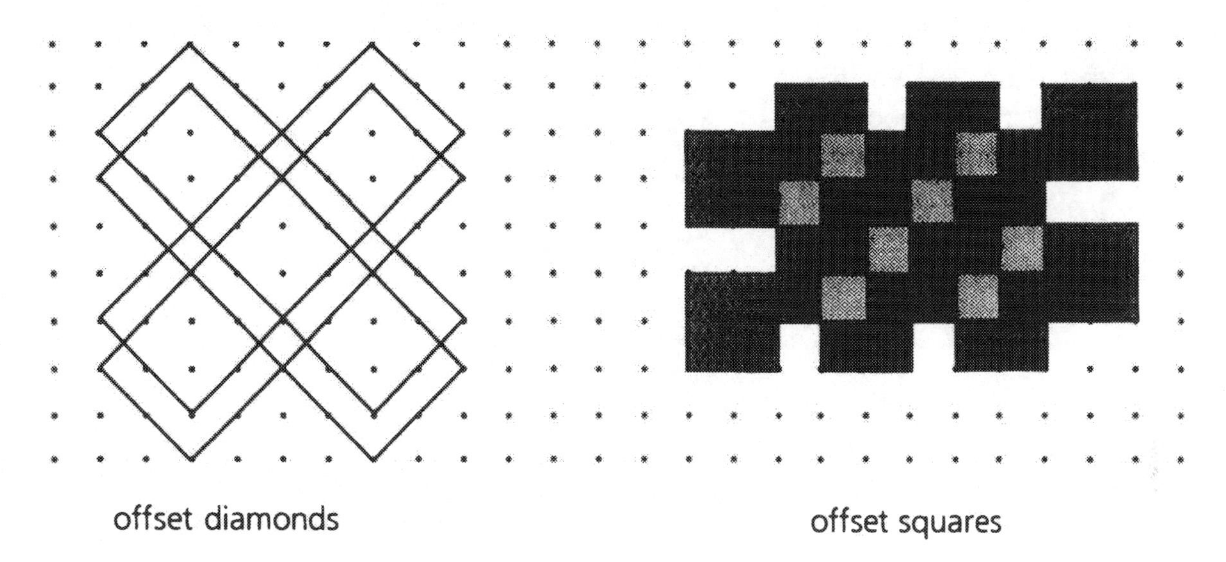

offset diamonds offset squares

Draw your own design using a simple shape. Then draw the same design in a position that is offset a small amount from the original design.

Name_______________________

Artists in our century are still using tessellations in their work. The most famous of these artists is M. C. Escher. By altering geometric shapes that tessellate, he created a wide variety of designs. Many of his creations are things in nature like fish, birds, or insects.

He would create a shape such as the one on the right. From this shape, he would draw something that looked like a real thing, such as an animal or person.

Be an artist like M. C. Escher. The shapes below were created by altering a square and will tessellate. Draw details inside each of the shapes to create an animal or person.

Note: There are many books on the art of M.C. Escher. Check your library for examples of his work.

Name________________________

You can modify a rectangle to form interesting tessellating shapes. A **translation** is a slide on a plane along the path of a straight line. Using this method, you can start at one corner of a rectangle and cut a free-flowing line along one side to the other corner. If you then slide that piece **straight** across to the opposite side, you will have a shape that will tessellate.

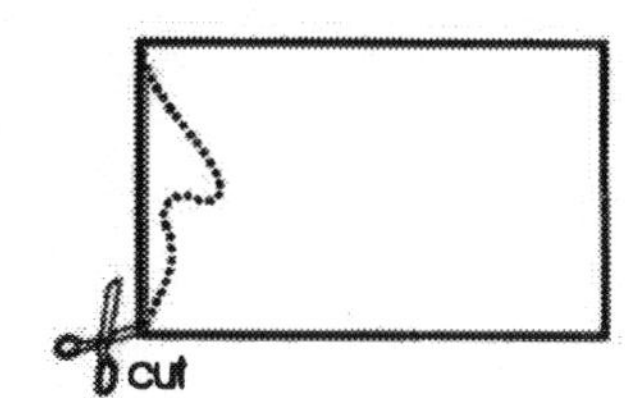

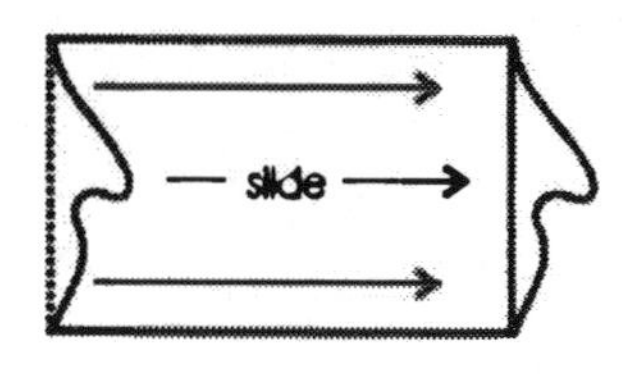

If you want a smaller cut than from corner to corner, you should draw straight lines across the rectangle to guide your cut and slide.

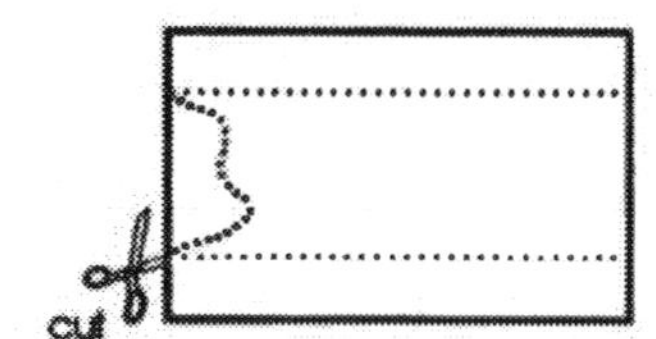

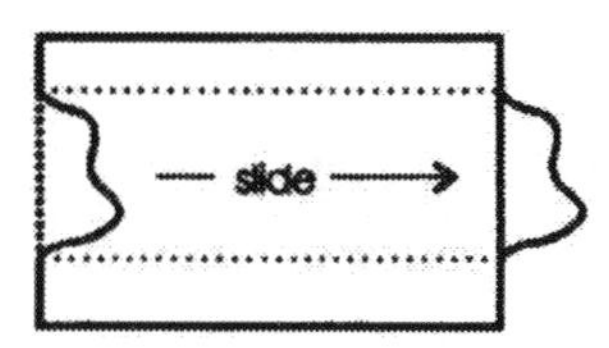

Materials

3" square (cut from tag board or manila folder), 3" x 15" strip of white construction paper, 4" x 16" strip of black construction paper

Procedure

1. Cut a piece from one side of the square as described above.
2. Slide the piece **straight across** the square as shown above.
3. Carefully tape the piece in place.
4. Place the pattern you have made at one end of the 3" x 15" drawing paper and trace around it.
5. Make a border design by repeating the pattern all the way across the strip. Then use your imagination to color a repeating design.
6. Mount your colored strip on the 4" x 16" strip of black paper.

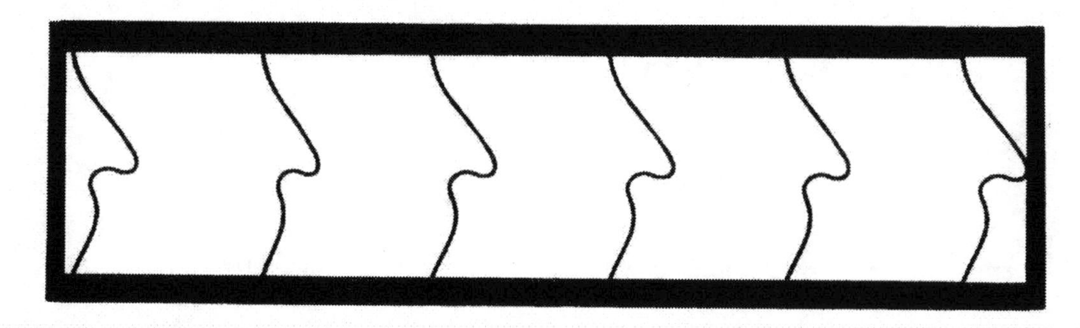

Name________________________

You can create a very interesting design using the cut and slide transformation to modify all four sides of a rectangle. An example is shown below.

Materials

3" manila or tag board square (or any rectangle), scrap paper, drawing paper (9" x 12" or smaller)

Procedure

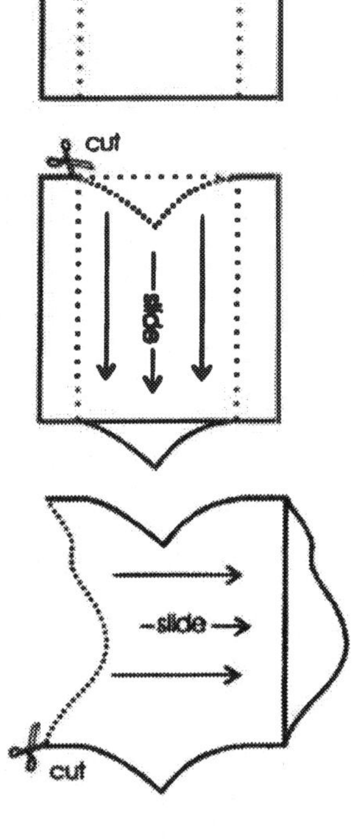

1. Cut a piece from the top side of your rectangle. Slide the piece **straight down** and carefully tape it in place at the bottom of the rectangle. Don't make your cuts too intricate or complicated.

2. Cut a piece from the left side of your rectangle. Slide the piece **straight across** and carefully tape it in place at the right side of the rectangle.

3. Trace around the pattern you have made 3 or 4 times on scrap paper. Imagine what picture you might make from the shape. Fill in the shapes with different images. Choose your favorite idea to use for your project.

4. Starting in one corner of the drawing paper, trace around your pattern until you have covered the page. Complete your Escher-type project by coloring in the shapes with your favorite design.

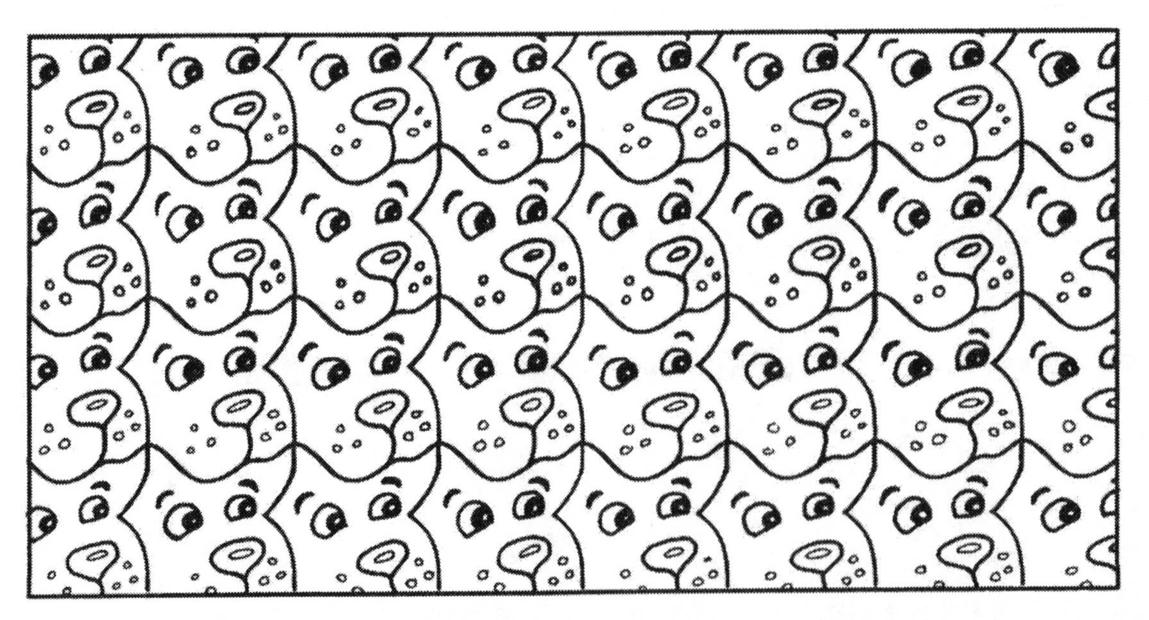

Name________________________

You can create a tessellating design from a triangle using the rotation technique by marking the **midpoints** of each side of your triangle, then cutting a piece from one half of one side of the triangle and **rotating** it 180° around the midpoint of that side.

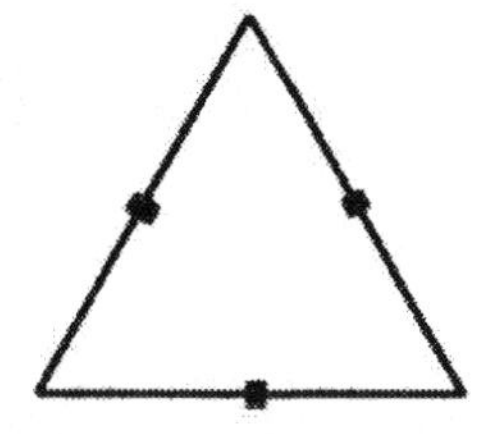

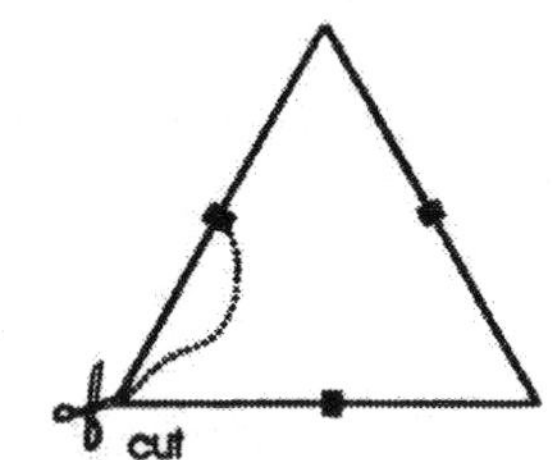

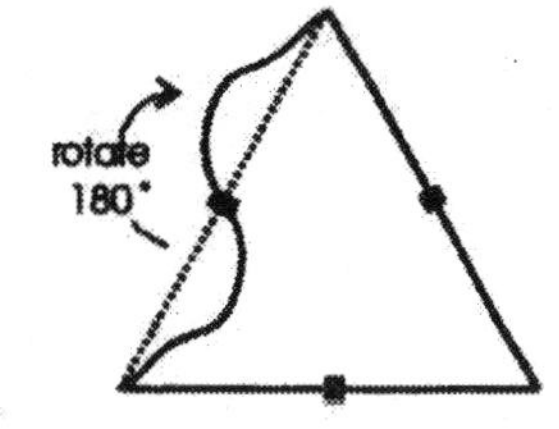

You can repeat this procedure with each side of the triangle, as shown below.

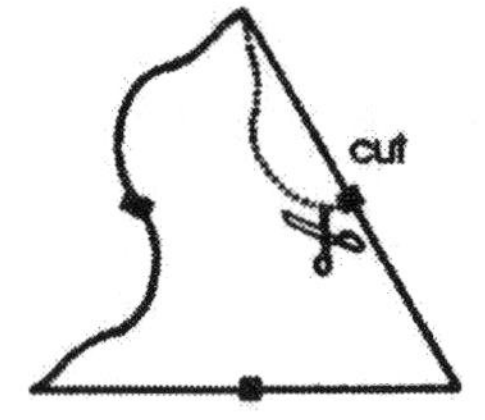

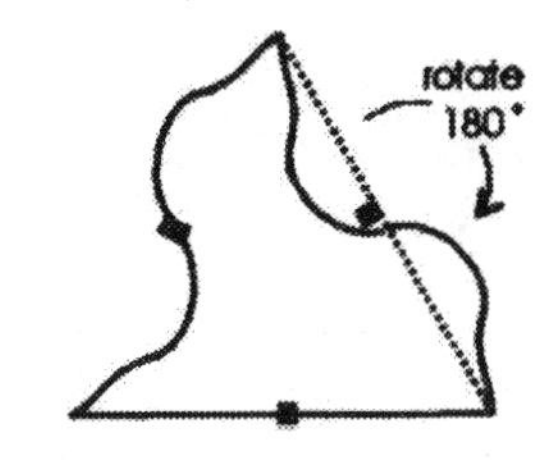

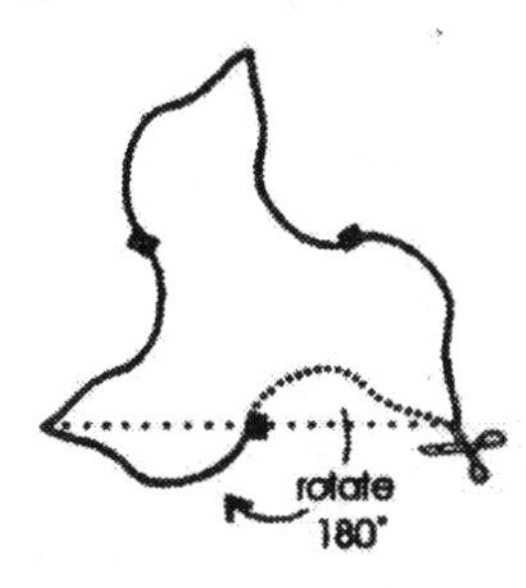

Materials

3" equilateral triangle (manila or tag board), ruler, scrap paper, 9" x 12" drawing paper

Procedure

1. Mark the midpoints on each side of the triangle and starting at the midpoint, cut a piece from one half of the side.
2. Rotate the piece 180° around the midpoint and carefully tape the piece in place, as shown above.
3. Repeat steps 1 and 2 with the other two sides of the triangle.
4. Trace around the pattern you have made 3 or 4 times on scrap paper and decide what picture you might make from it.
5. Starting in one corner of the drawing paper, trace around your pattern until you have covered the page. Complete your Escher-type project by coloring the shapes using your favorite design idea.

Name______________________

A **number line** can be extended as long as you wish to make it. It can extend on and on without an end. We often show this by using an arrow at one or both ends.

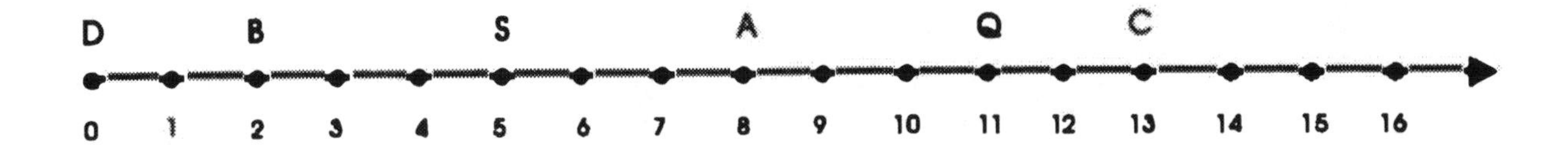

On a horizontal number line, a given number is less than those to the right and greater than those to the left. Point Q represents a number that is greater than the number represented by point S. Every point on the line corresponds to a number called its **coordinate**.

1. What are the coordinates for each of these points on the number line above?

   A______ B______ C______ D______

The number line on the right is a vertical number line. A given number on a vertical number line is greater that those below it and less than those above it. Every point on the line corresponds to a number called its **coordinate**.

2. What is the coordinate for each of these points on the number line to the right?

   E______ F______

   G______ H______

   I______ J______

15
14
13
G 12
11
H 10
9
F 8
7
I 6
5
E 4
3
J 2
1
0

DOI: 10.4324/9781003235026-6

Name________________________

A **plane** is a flat surface. We can locate specific points on a plane by using **coordinates** on number lines.

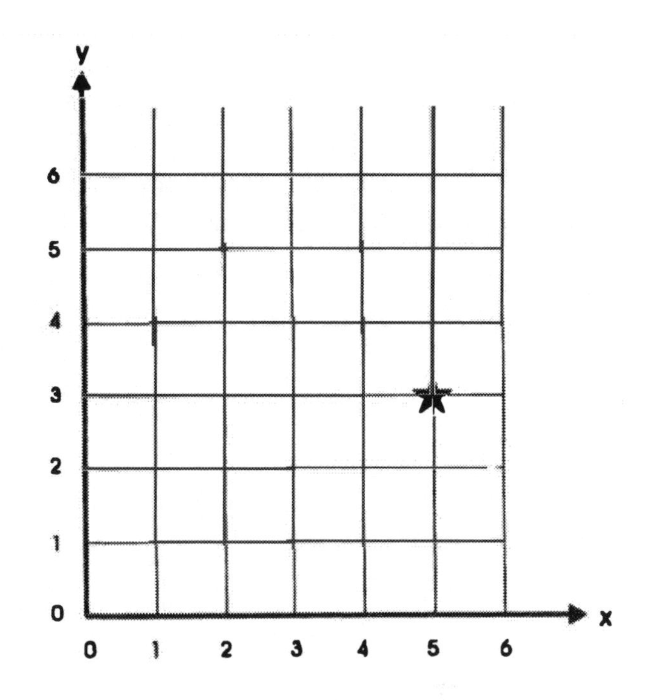

Look at the number lines to the right. The number line marked with an X is called the **X axis** and extends horizontally from zero (0). The number line marked Y is called the **Y axis** and extends vertically from zero. Put a red ● where the 0 on the X axis meets 0 on the Y axis. That is the point (0, 0).

Find the point on the X axis that corresponds to 5. Find the point on the Y axis that corresponds to 3. Find the point on the grid where those coordinates intersect. The location of the ★ on the grid can be shown by the coordinates (5, 3).

When using a coordinate system to indicate the location of a point, the horizontal axis (X axis) appears first and the vertical axis (Y axis) is second. The order is very important. The location of (3, 5) is different from (5, 3). Find the point (3, 5) on the grid above and make a ■ at that point.

Grids can be used for graphing. On the graph below the X axis shows the number of weeks. The Y axis shows the number of words correct on a weekly spelling test. Record the test scores for each week by putting a dot in the correct place on the grid. Then use a ruler to connect the dots.

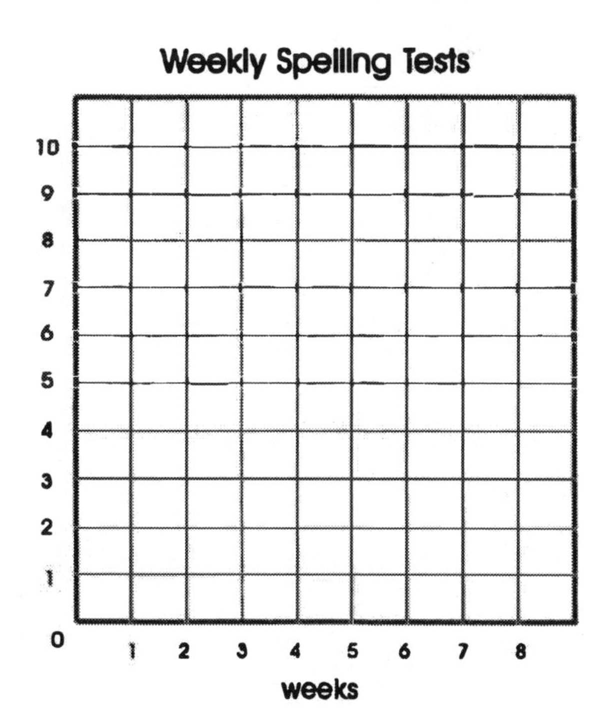

Week	Correct	Coordinate Pairs
1	7	(1, 7)
2	9	(2, 9)
3	7	(3, 7)
4	8	(4, ___)
5	9	________
6	7	________
7	9	________
8	10	________

Name______________________

The location of any place on a map can be described by using ordered pairs of numbers. For example, the location of Lake Love on the map below can be indicated by the coordinates (10, 6). The order of the numbers indicates on which axis each coordinate is located. The **horizontal axis** is listed first, followed by the **vertical axis**.

1. Write the ordered pairs that describe the location of each place listed below.

Place	**Coordinates**
Sweet City	________
Heart Lake	________
Mt. Cupid	________
Honeyville	________
Darling Creek joins Romance River	________
Liebeburg	________

2. Draw two more features on the map and list the coordinates.

______________________________ ______________________________

Arrow Island

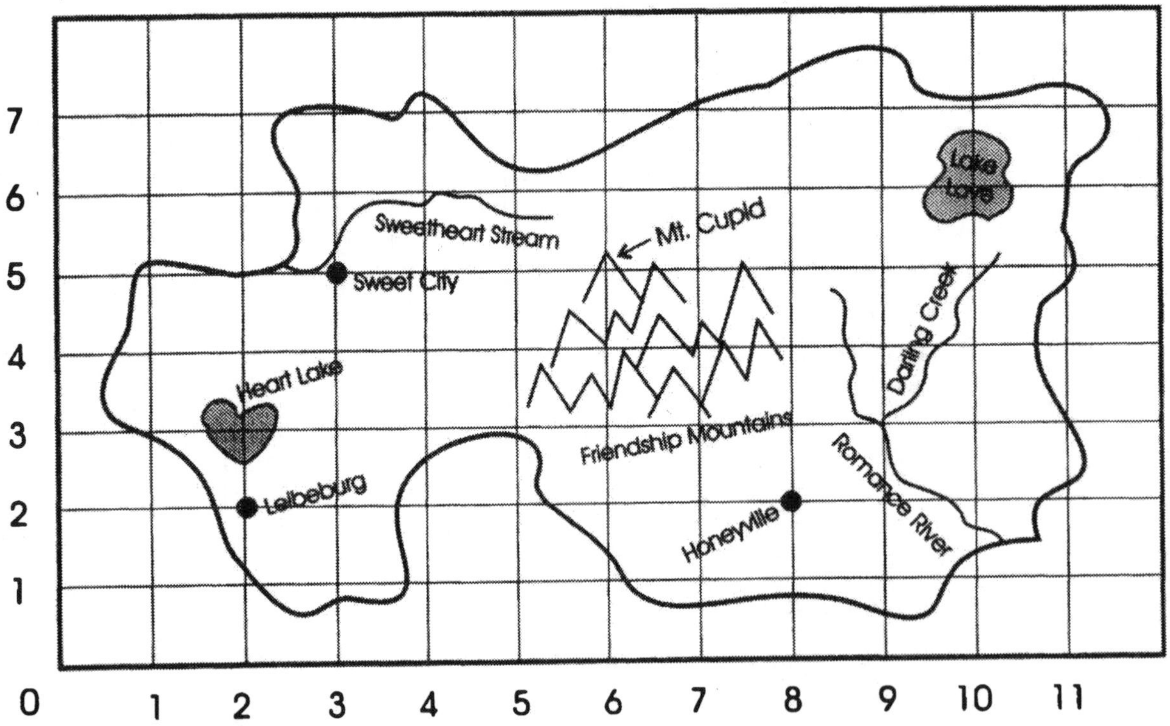

Name________________________

The X and Y coordinates shown in the chart below can be written as ordered pairs. An X value of 1 and a Y value of 2 is written as (1, 2).

1. Look for a pattern in the numbers in the chart. Then extend the pattern to fill in the chart. Mark the location of these coordinates on the graph. Use a ruler to connect the points.

X	Y	Coordinates
0	0	(0, 0)
1	2	(1, 2)
2	4	(2, 4)
3	6	(3, 6)
4	8	________
___	___	________
___	___	________
___	___	________

2. Find the pattern in this chart. Extend the pattern to complete the chart. Write each pair as an ordered pair. Graph these ordered pairs on the graph above. Use a ruler to connect the points.

X	Y	Coordinates
15	5	(15, 5)
12	4	________
___	___	________
___	___	________
___	___	________
___	___	________

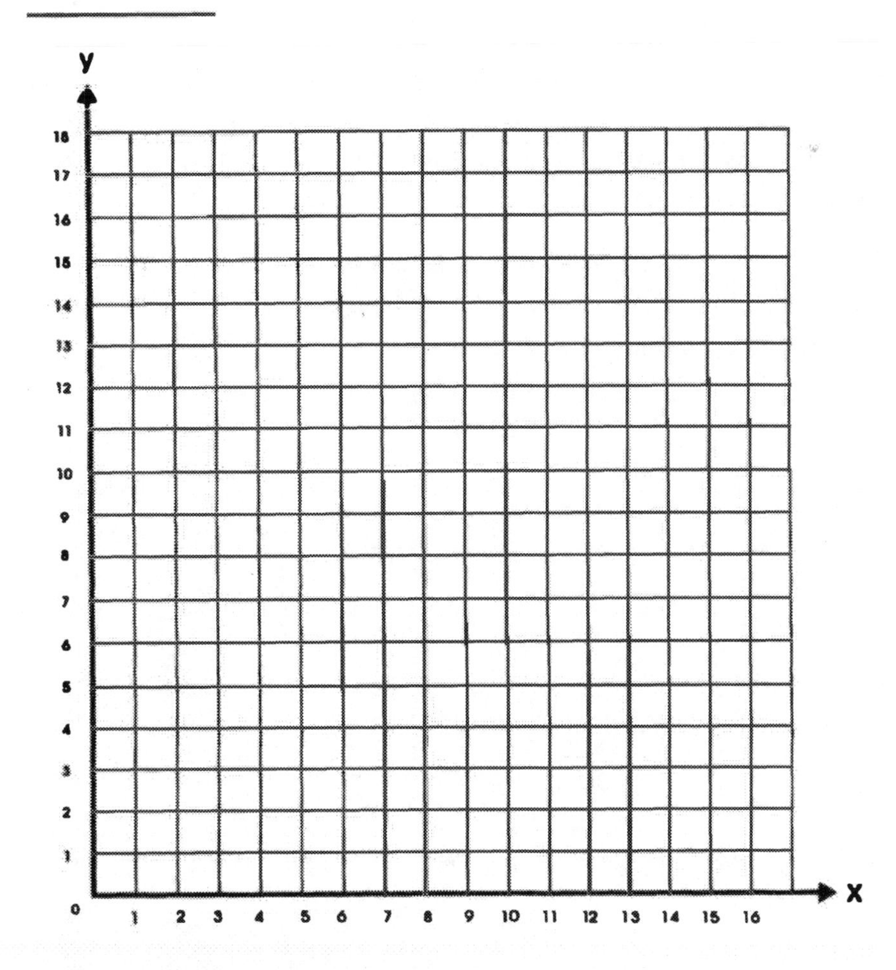

Above and Below Zero

Name______________________

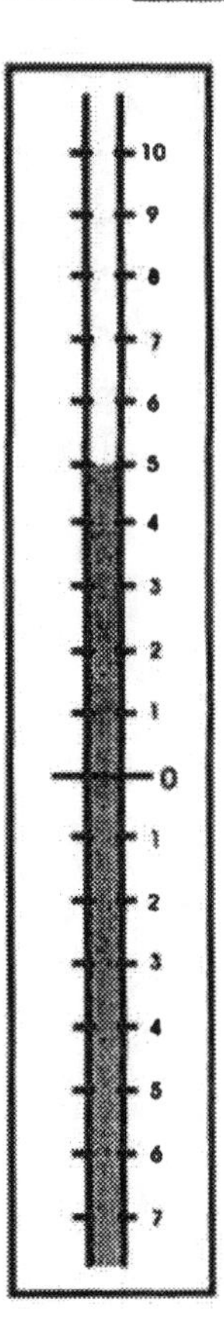

When reading a thermometer, we know that the warmer it is, the higher above zero the temperature will be. This thermometer shows a temperature of only 5° above zero. If it got 5° colder, the temperature would be 0°. If it dropped another 5°, then the temperature would be 5° below zero or –5°.

We write temperature below zero with a negative sign before the number to show that it is below zero. How would you write the temperature that is:

a. 1 degree below 0°? ______________

b. 3 degrees below 0°? ______________

c. 6 degrees below 5°? ______________

d. 9 degrees below 5°? ______________

e. 12 degrees below 5°? ______________

f. 3 degrees above –10°? ______________

A number line that shows integers (positive and negative numbers) extends continuously in both directions. On a horizontal number line, the numbers to the right of zero are **positive**. A + sign or no sign in front of a number means that it is a positive number or a number greater than zero.

Numbers to the left of zero are **negative** numbers. A minus (–) sign in front of a number means that it is a negative number or a number that is less than zero. Negative 4 is written as –4 and means that it is 4 units less than zero.

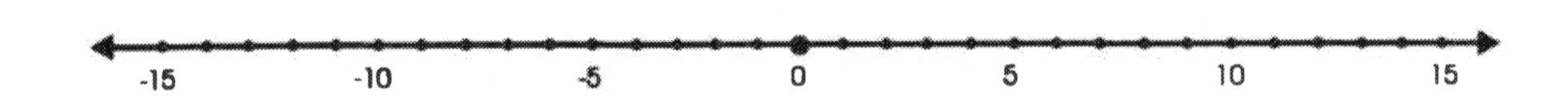

Mark the following numbers on the number line.

g. –3 h. 7 i. –13 j. 10 k. –6 l. –9 m. 1 n. 5 o. –11

Name_______________________

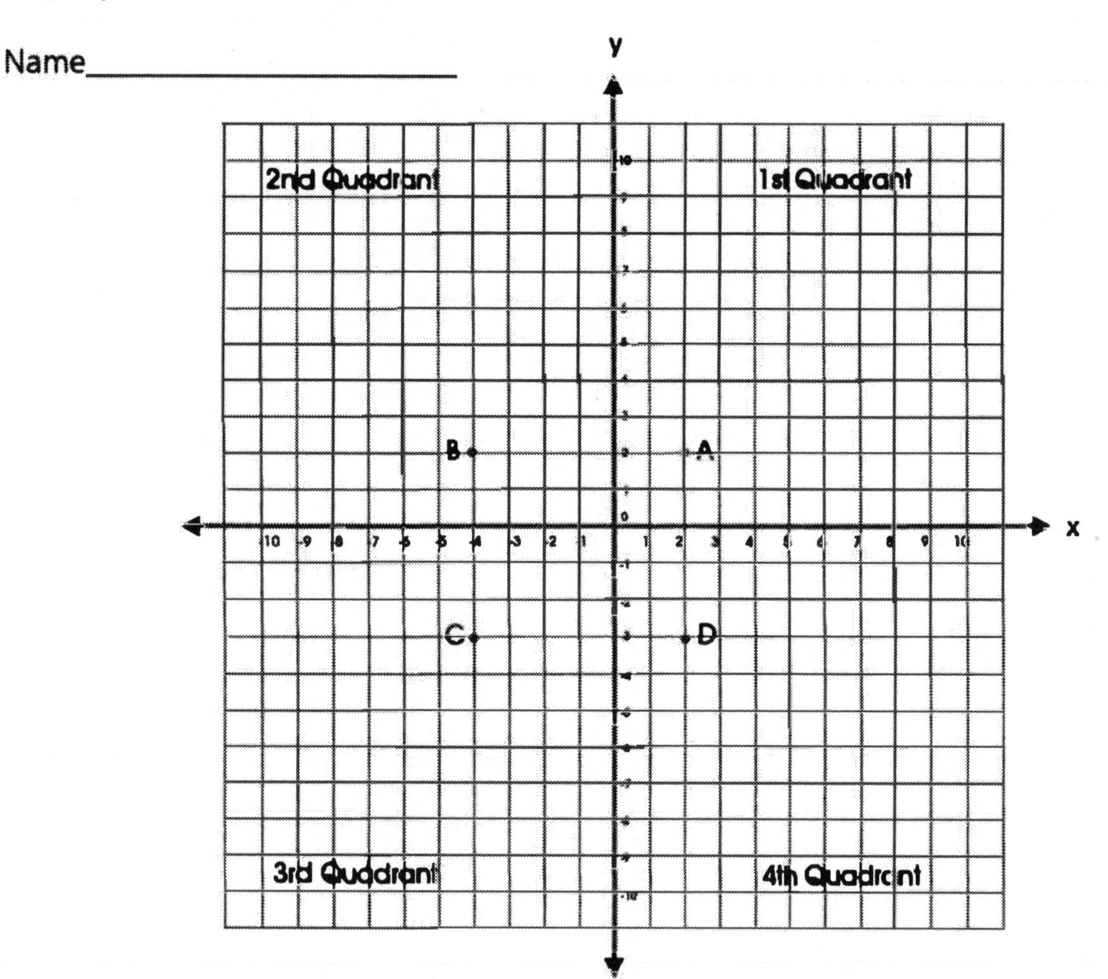

The horizontal and vertical number lines intersect to form right angles at the point that corresponds to zero on both number lines. The X axis and the Y axis divide the area into four parts called **quadrants.**

We can find any point on a graph by naming the coordinates of that point. These coordinates are **ordered pairs** of numbers. Remember that the first number in the pair indicates the location on the horizontal (X) axis, and the second number indicates the vertical (Y) coordinate. Therefore, (2, –3) would be where D is in the 4th quadrant, and (–4, 2) would be where the B is in the 2nd quadrant.

1. What is the location of point A in the 1st quadrant? _______________
2. What is the location of point C in the 3rd quadrant? _______________
3. In which quadrant would each of the following points be located?

a. (6, 7) _______________

b. (6, –7) _______________

c. (–8, 5) _______________

d. (–6, –7) _______________

e. (–6, 7) _______________

f. (–4, –2) _______________

Designs in Four Quadrants

Name ______________________

A simple shape has been graphed in each of the four quadrants. Put a point on the graph for each ordered pair and draw line segments to connect each point. Connect point A to point B, point B to point C, and so forth.

First Quadrant

A. (0, 6)
B. (8, 1)
C. (5, 9)
D. (2, 1)
E. (10, 6)
F. (0, 6)

Second Quadrant

A. (–3, 9)
B. (–10, 9)
C. (–10, 2)
D. (–3, 9)
E. (–3, 2)
F. (–10, 2)

Third Quadrant

A. (–6, –1)
B. (–10, –9)
C. (–2, –10)
D. (–6, –1)
E. (–5, 0)
F. (–1, –9)
G. (–2, –10)

Fourth Quadrant

A. (2, –3)
B. (8, –3)
C. (10, –6)
D. (0, –6)
E. (2, –3)

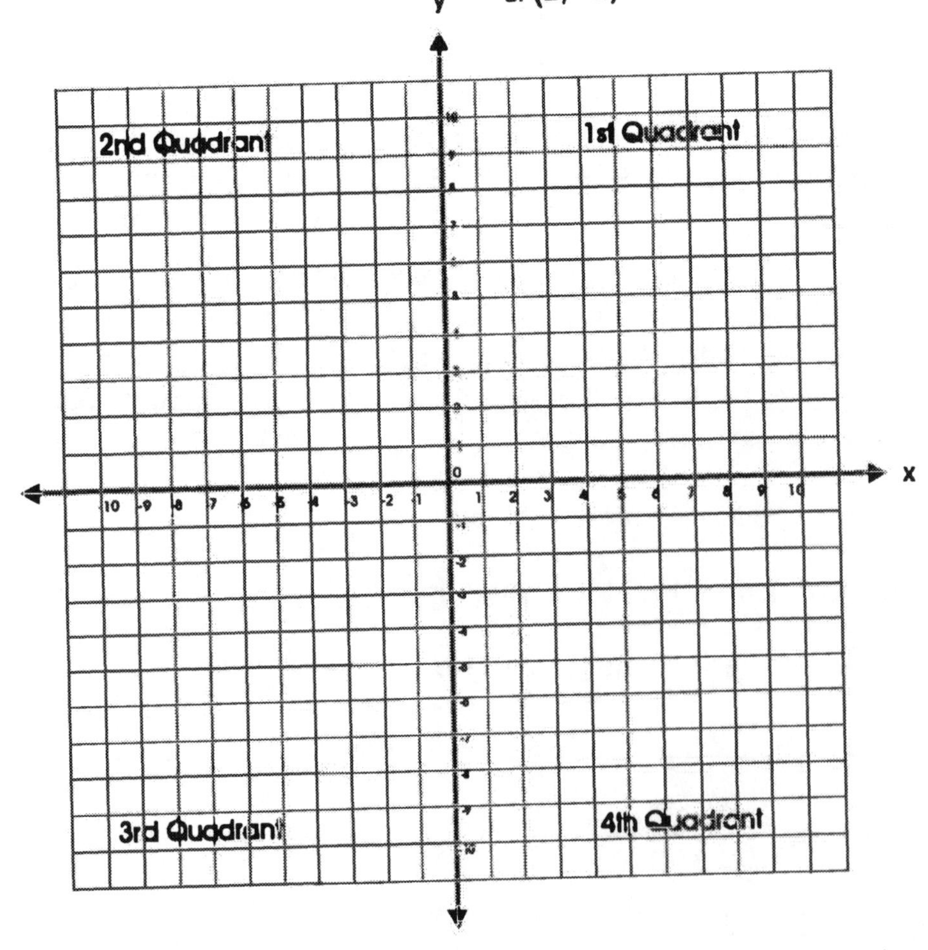

Name_______________________

Graph each ordered pair in the given sequence. Connect the points (in sequence) to make a picture.

(−5, −10) start

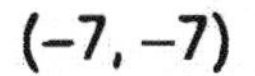

(−7, −7)	(−5, 6)
(−3, −5)	(−1, 6)
(0, −5)	(5, 3)
(1, −4)	(7, 1)
(−1, 6)	(9, −2)
(3, 7)	(9, −4)
(−2, 10)	(3, −10) finish

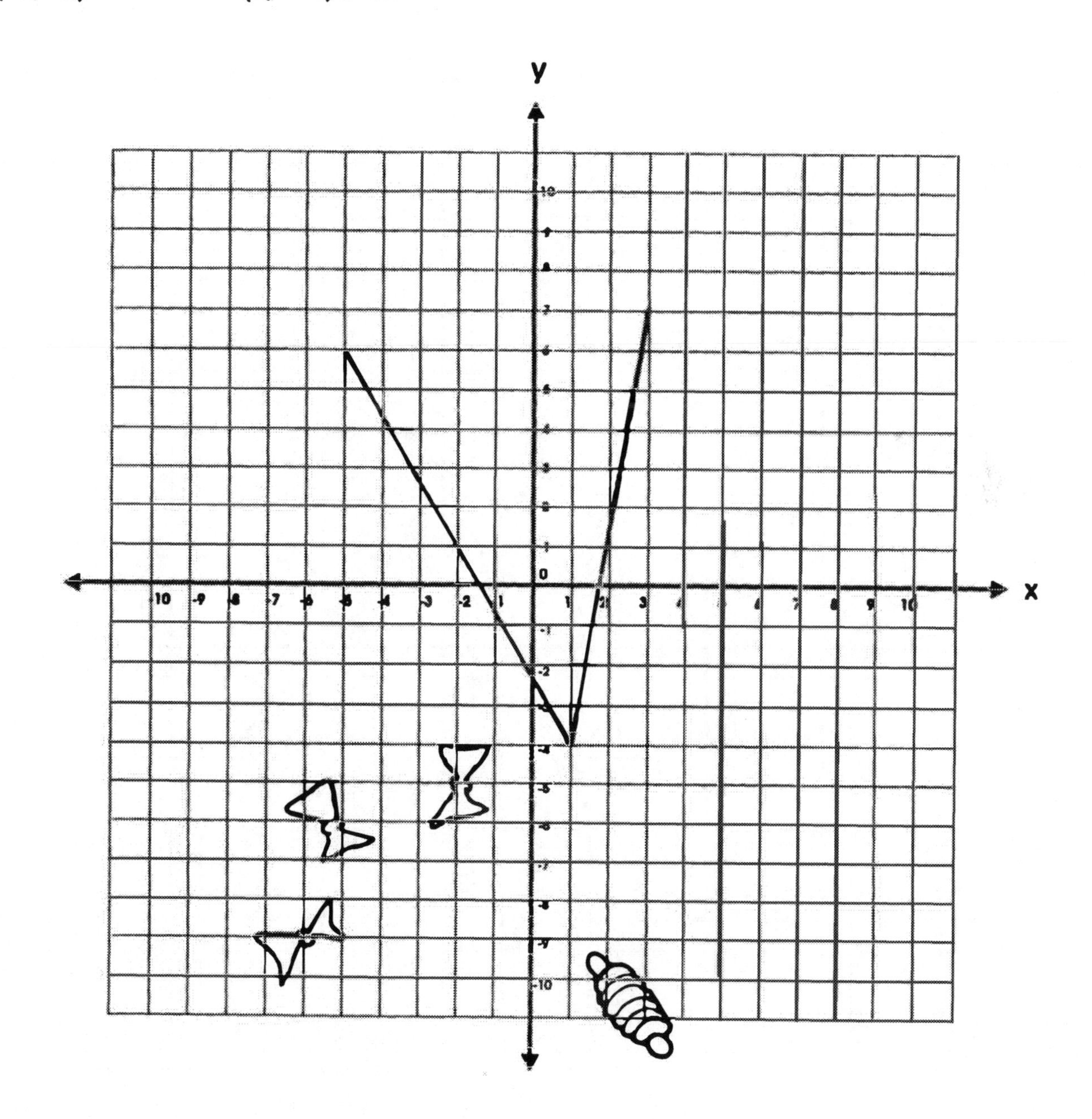

Name________________________

Graph each ordered pair in the given sequence. Connect the points (in sequence) to make a picture.

Line 1
(12, 2) start
(12, –12)
(–8, –12)
(–8, 2)
(–7, 2)
(–7, 5)
(–6, 5)
(–4, 8)
(–2, 5)
(–1, 5)
(–1, 2) finish

Line 2
(0, 2) start
(0, 5)
(1, 5)
(3, 8)
(5, 5)
(6, 5)
(6, 2) finish

Line 3
(7, 2) start
(7, 5)
(8, 5)
(10, 8)
(12, 5)
(13, 5)
(13, 2)
(14, 3)
(14, –11)
(12, –12) finish

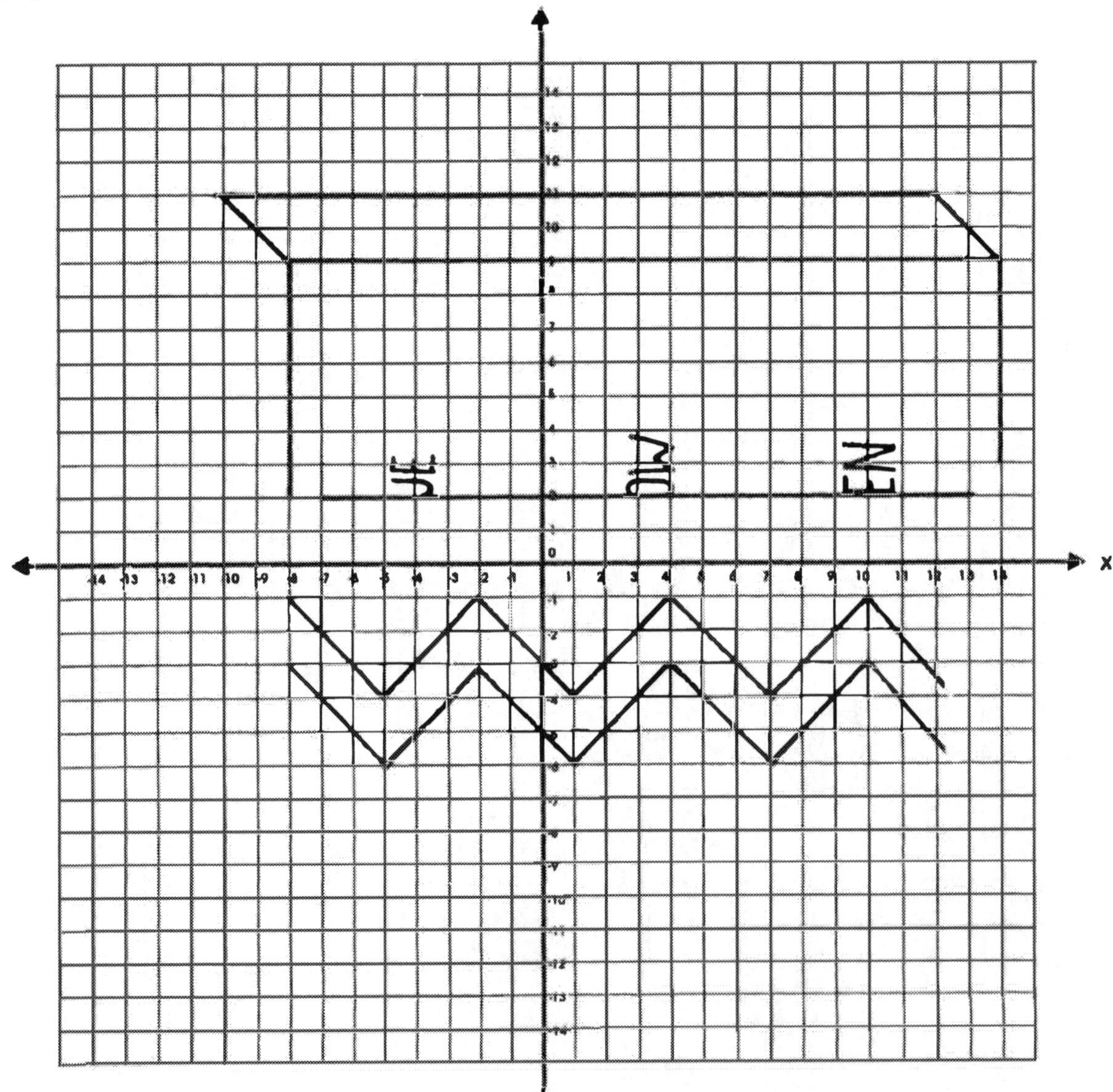

Name______________________

Graph each ordered pair in the given sequence. Connect the points (in sequence) to make a picture.

Line 1

(–8, 1) start
(–8, 2)
(0, –4)
(8, 2)
(4, 1)
(–4, 1)
(–8, 2)
(–4, 4)
(–4, 7)
(–3, 8)
(–3, 4)
(–2, 4)
(–2, 7)
(–1, 8)
(–1, 4)
(1, 4)
(1, 7)
(2, 8)
(2, 4)
(3, 4)
(3, 7)
(4, 8)
(4, 4)
(8, 2) finish

Line 2

(8, 2) start
(8, –8)
(–8, –8)
(–8, 1)
(0, –5)
(8, 1) finish

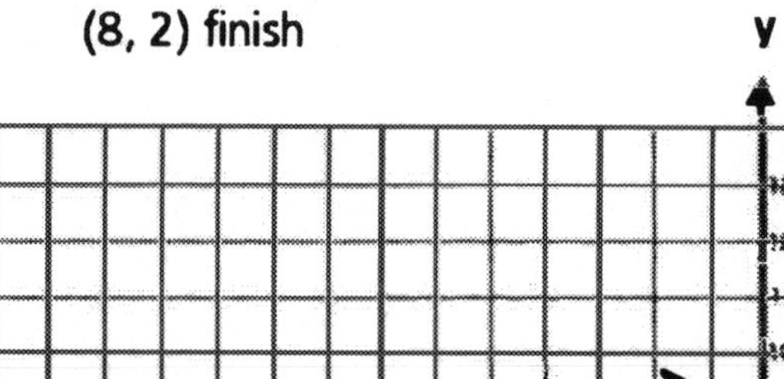

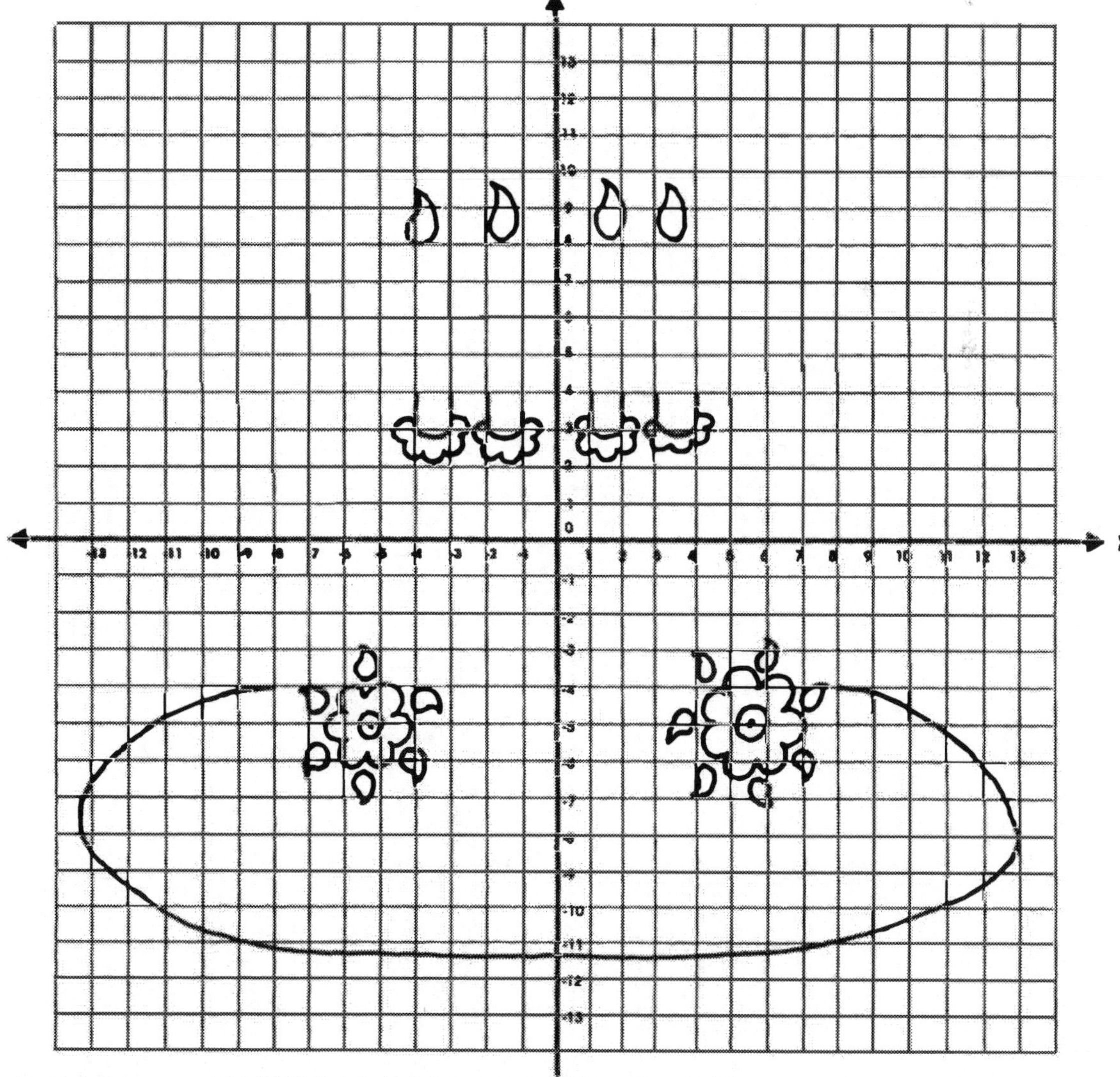

Name______________________

Graph each ordered pair in the given sequence. Connect the points (in sequence) to make a picture.

Line 1

(–13, 4) start
(–14, 2)
(–13, 0)
(–11, 1)
(–8, 0)
(–7, 2)
(–8, 5)
(–9, 6)
(–11, 6) finish

Line 2

(–8, 0) start
(–6, –2)
(–7, –4)
(–7, –6)
(–6, –8)
(–5, –7)
(–4, –8)
(–3, –7)
(–2, –8)
(–2, –5)
(–6, –2) finish

Line 3

(–2, –5) start
(1, –5)
(4, –4)
(4, –6)
(6, –8)
(7, –7)
(9, –7)
(9, –6)
(10 –5)
(7, –4)
(4, –4) finish

Line 4

(7, –4) start
(11, 0)
(13, 0)
(14, 2)
(11, 1)
(9, 2)
(7, 4)
(5, 5)
(3, 6)
(1, 6)
(–2, 5)
(–7, 2) finish

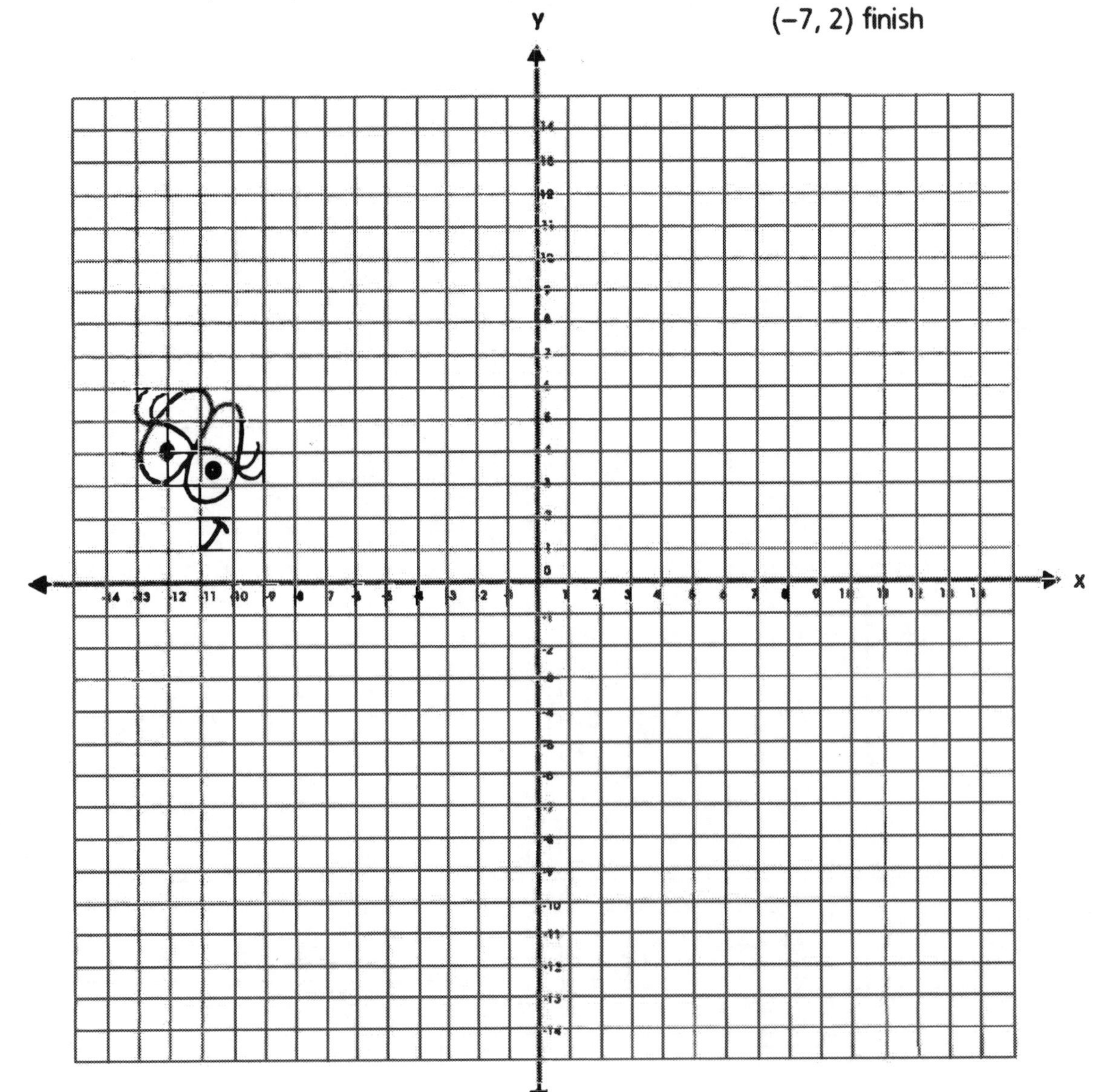

Name__________________________

Graph each ordered pair in the given sequence. Connect the points (in sequence) to make a picture.

Line 1

(−1, −2) start
(−6, −2)
(−6, −1)
(−8, −1)
(−8, −2)
(−10, −2)
(−10, 0)
(−9, 1)
(−7, 1)
(−7, 4)
(−3, 4)
(−3, −1)
(−1, −1) finish

Line 2

(−1, −2) start
(1, −2)
(1, −1)
(3, −1)
(3, −2)
(8, −2)
(8, −1)
(10, −1)
(10, −2)
(13, −2)
(9, 5)
(2, 5)
(1, 6)
(−1, 6)
(−1, −2) finish

Line 3

(−6, 1) start
(−6, 3)
(−5, 3)
(−4, 1)
(−6, 1) finish

Line 4

(7, 0) start
(11, 5)
(13, 5)
(14, 2)
(11, 2)
(11, 5) finish

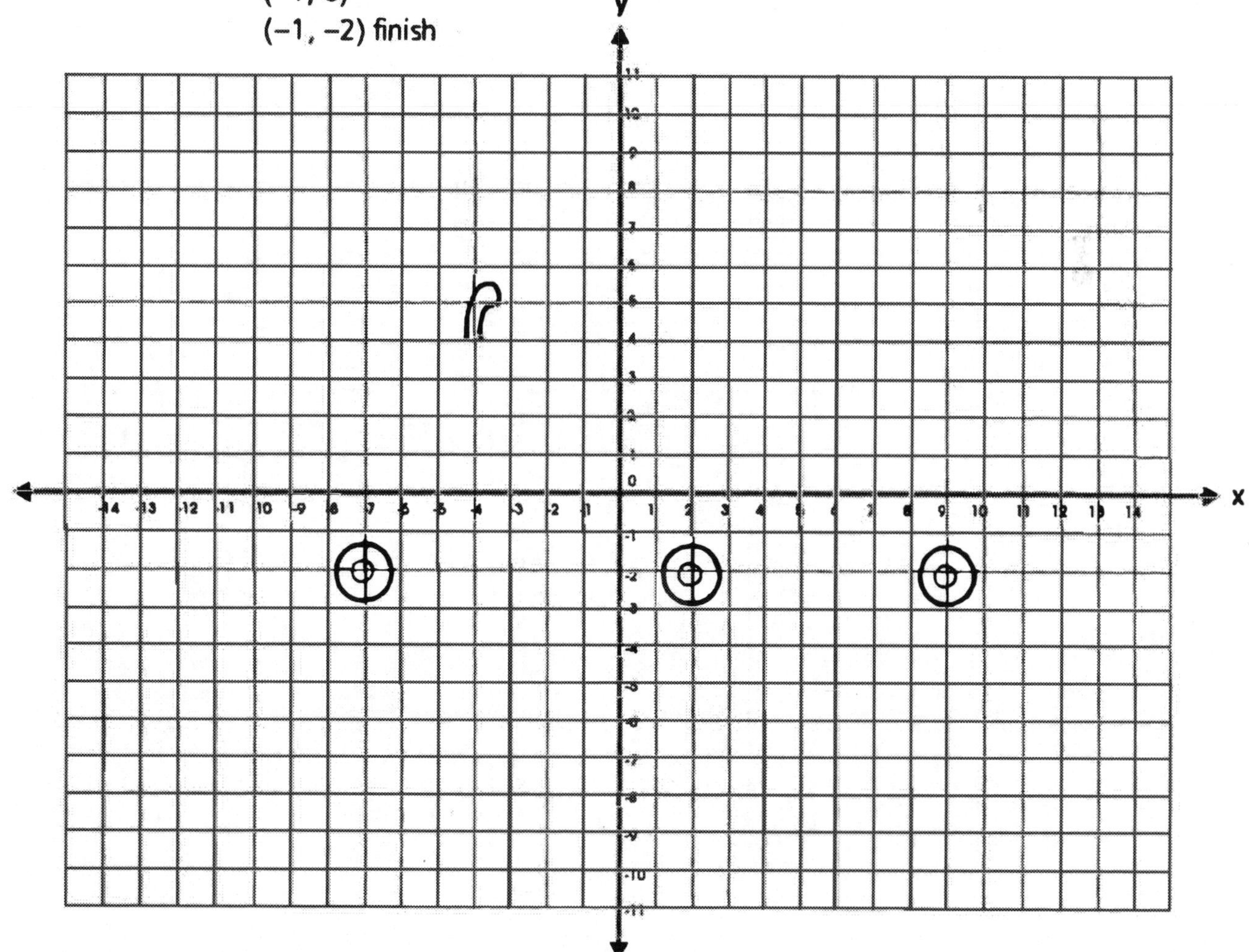

Name________________________

Graph each ordered pair in the given sequence. Connect the points (in sequence) to make a picture.

Line 1
(–1, –11) start
(–2, –9)
(–1, –9)
(–1, –6)
(–12, –6)
(–7, 1)
(–8, 1)
(–3, 7)
(–4, 7)
(0, 12)
(4, 7)
(3, 7)
(8, 1)
(7, 1)
(12, –6)
(1, –6)
(1, –9)
(2, –9)
(1, –11)
(–1, –11) finish

Line 2
(–6, –11) start
(–9, –11)
(–9, –8)
(–6, –8)
(–6, –11)
(–3, –11)
(–3, –8)
(–5, –8)
(–5, –11) finish

Line 3
(4, –8) start
(3, –8)
(3, –11)
(6, –11)
(6, –8)
(5, –8) finish

Line 4
(10, –7) start
(9, –6)
(10, –6)
(9, –7)
(11, –7)
(11, –11)
(8, –11)
(8, –7)
(9, –7) finish

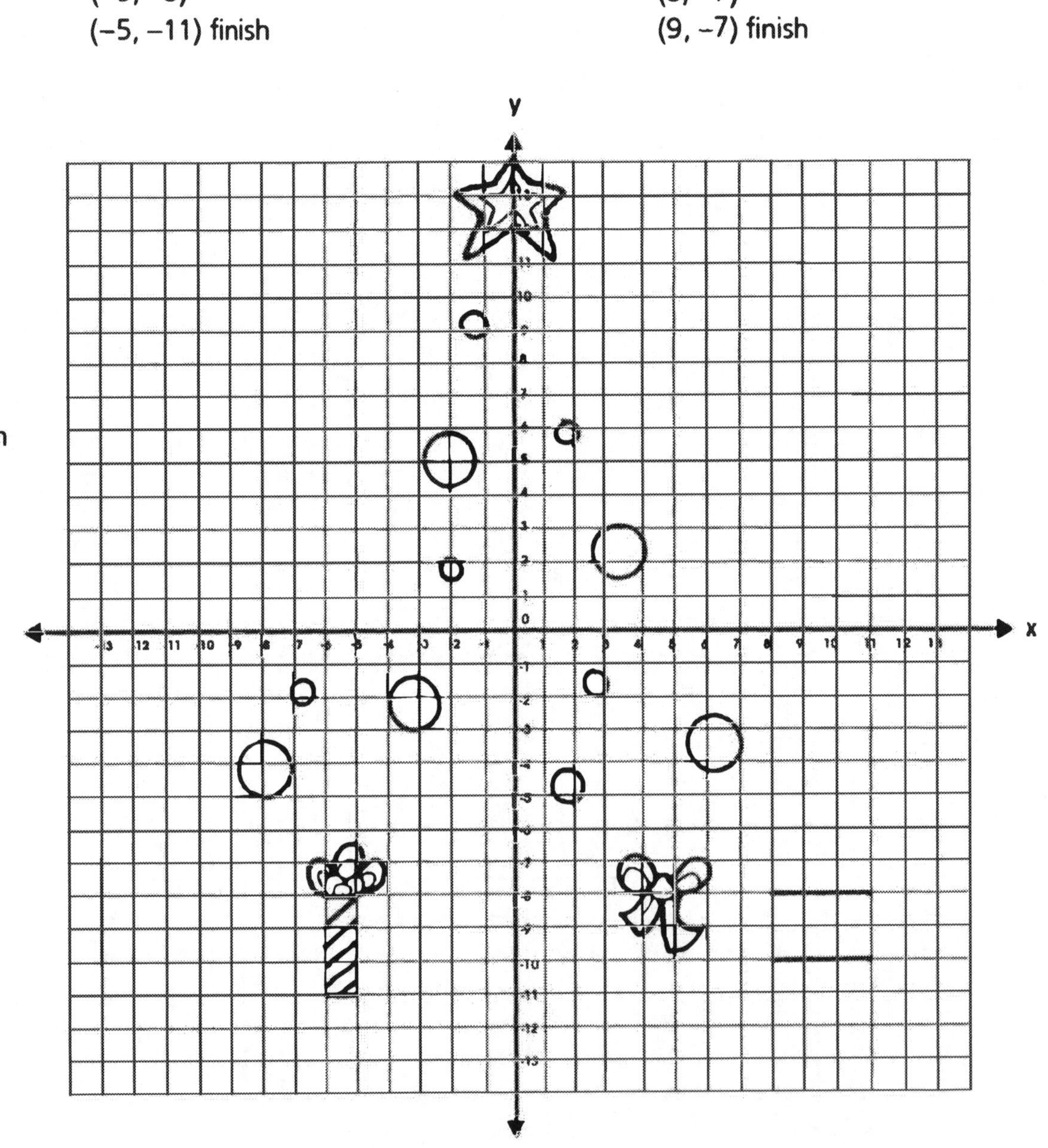

Name________________________

Graph each ordered pair in the given sequence. Connect the points (in sequence) to make a picture.

Line 1
(−11, −12) start
(−14, −12)
(−14, 2)
(−11, 2)
(−11, 5)
(−10, 5)
(−10, 7)
(−7, 7)
(−7, 5)
(−6, 5)
(−6, 2)
(−3, 2)
(−3, −12)
(−5, −12) finish

Line 2
(−1, −12) start
(−1, 5)
(0, 5)
(0, 6)
(1, 6)
(1, 8)
(3, 8)
(3, 6)
(4, 6)
(4, 5)
(5, 5)
(5, −12)
(−1, −12) finish

Line 3
(5, −1) start
(7, −1)
(7, 2)
(9, 5)
(11, 2)
(11, −1)
(13, −1)
(13, −12)
(5, −12) finish

Line 4
(−10, −3) start
(−10, −4)
(−7, −4)
(−7, −3)
(−10, −3) finish

Line 5
(−11, −12)
(−11, −8)
(−5, −8)
(−5, −12)
(−11, −12) finish

Line 6
(8, 0) start
(9, 2)
(10, 0)
(9, −2)
(8, 0) finish

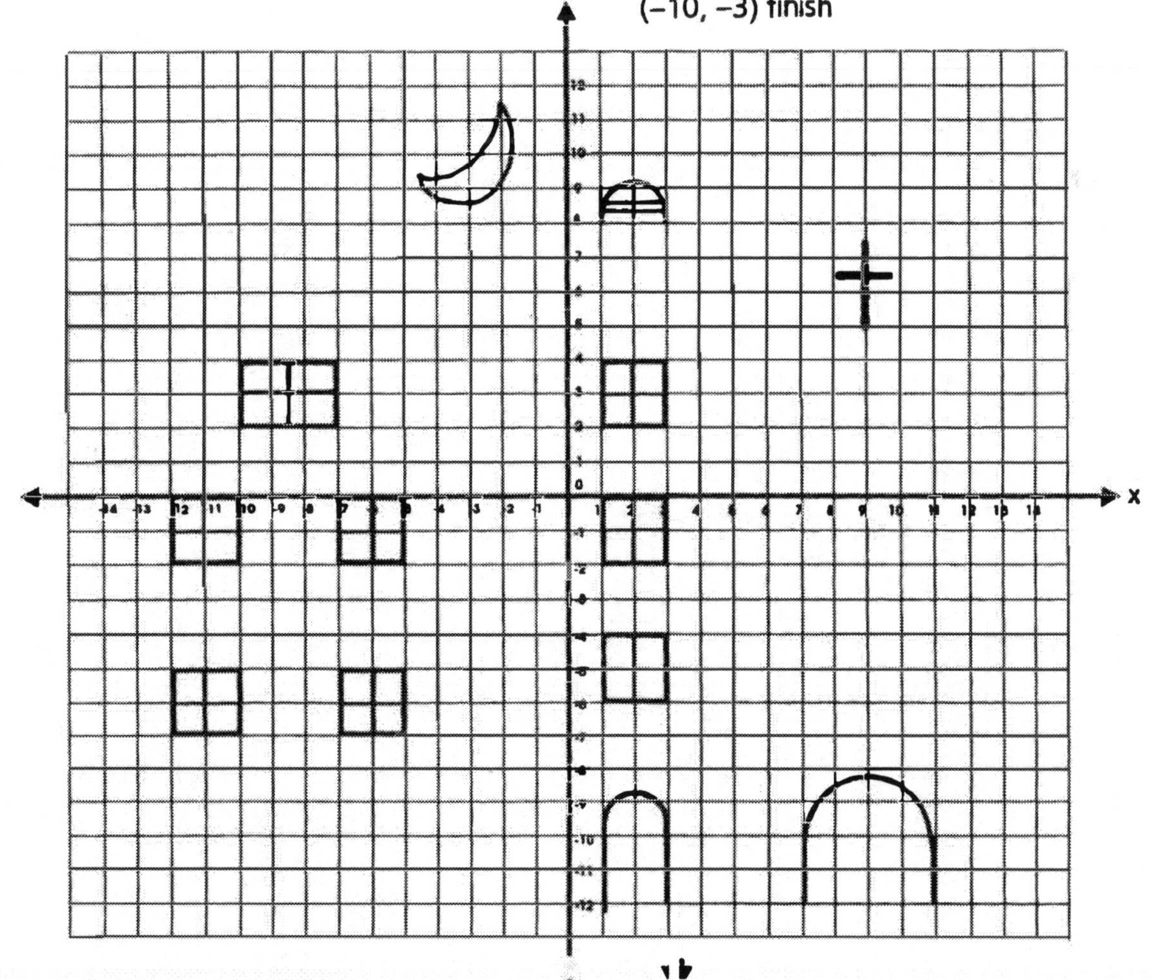

Name____________________________

Make a colorful geometric design by graphing the coordinate pairs below. Use a ruler to connect the points in each sequence in the color indicated.

red

(0,12) start
(11, −8)
(−11, −8)
(0, 12) finish

(−11, 8) start
(11, 8)
(0, −12)
(−11, 8) finish

green

(−11, 8) start
(0, 12)
(11, 8)
(14, 0)
(11, −8)
(0, −12)
(−11, −8)
(−14, 0
(−11, 8) finish

purple

(−11, −8) start
(11, 8) finish

(−11, 8) start
(11, −8) finish

blue

(−14, 0) start
(11, 8)
(11, −8)
(−14, 0) finish

(−11, −8) start
(−11, 8)
(14, 0)
(−11, −8) finish

Answers

Line Drawings

Answers are correct if lines follow the established pattern.

Combinations and Permutations

Lesson 1 - page 19

1. Alan-Burt, Alan-Charlie, Alan-Darren, Burt-Charlie, Burt-Darren, Charlie, Darren - 6 combinations

Lesson 2 - pg. 20

1. 6 ways; car-subway, car-bus, walk-subway, walk-bus, bike-subway, walk-bus
2. $\overline{AB}$, $\overline{AC}$, $\overline{AD}$, $\overline{BC}$, $\overline{BD}$, $\overline{CD}$ - 6 lines

Lesson 3 - page 21

1. clam-seahorse, clam-octopus, clam-fish, clam-whale, seahorse-octopus, seahorse-fish, seahorse-whale, octopus-fish, octopus-whale, fish-whale
2. 6-6, 6-5, 6-4, 6-3, 6-2, 6-1, 6-0
   5-5, 5-4, 5-3, 5-2, 5-1, 5-0
   4-4, 4-3, 4-2, 4-1, 4-0
   3-3, 3-2, 3-1, 3-0
   2-2, 2-1, 2-0
   1-1, 1-0
   0-0; total 28 pieces

Lesson 4 - page 22

1. one fruit - strawberries, bananas, grapes, peaches - total 4
   two fruits - s-b, s-g, s-p, b-g, b-p, g-p - total 6
   three fruits - s-b-g, s-g-p, s-b-p, b-g-p - total 4
   four fruits - s-b-g-p - total 1
2. Let P stand for pants and S stand for sweater
   P1-S1, P1-S2, P1-S3
   P2-S1, P2-S2, P2-S3
   P3-S1, P3-S2, P3-S3
   P4-S1, P4-S2, P4-S3
   P5-S1, P5-S2, P5-S3; 15 combinations

Lesson 5 - page 23

1. L1-R1, L1-L2, L1-R2, L1-L3, L1-R3, R1-L2, R1-R2, R1-L3, R1-R3, L2-R2, L2-L3, L2-R3, R2-L3, R2-R3, L3-R3 - 15 combinations
2. 45 combinations; 5 matching pairs

Lesson 6 - page 24

1. E= English, M= math, S= science, G= geography, SP= spelling
   E-M, E-S, E-G, E-SP, M-S, M-G, M-SP, S-G, S-SP, G-SP; 10 combinations
2. R= red, W= white, Y= yellow, Bl = black, T= tan, B = blue
   R-Bl, R-T, R-B, W-BL, W-T, W-B, Y-BL, Y-T, Y-B;
   9 combinations

Lesson 7 - page 25

1. 15 bows
2. R = red, B = blue, G = green, Y = yellow, P = purple
   RBGY, RBGP, RBYP, RGYP, BGYP - 5 combinations

Lesson 26 - page 26

1. 246, 264, 426, 462, 624, 642
2. piano- - sing-dance
   piano dance - sing
   dance - piano - sing
   dance - sing - piano
   sing - dance - piano
   sing - piano - dance

Lesson 9 - page 27

1. Zoey-Ziggy-Zac, Zoey-Zac-Ziggy
   Ziggy-Zac-Zoey, Ziggy-Zoey-Zac
   Zac-Zoey-Ziggy, Zac-Ziggy-Zoey
2. V= vanilla, C = chocolate, P = peach
   V-V, V-C; V-P, C-C. C-V, C-P, P-P, P-V, P-C

Lesson 10 - page 28

1. S= science, M= math, R = reading, Sp = spelling
   S-M-R, S-R-M, S-M-Sp, S-SP-M, S-R-Sp, S-SP-R, M-S-R, M-R-S, M-R-Sp, M-Sp-R, M-S-Sp, M-Sp-S, R-S-M, R-M-S, R-M-Sp, R-Sp-M, R-S-Sp, R-Sp-S, Sp-S-M, Sp-M-S, Sp-R-M. Sp-R-M, Sp-R-S, Sp-S-R - total of 24 permutations
2. Let A, B and C stand for the people.
   ABC, ACB, BAC, BCA, CAB, CBA

Lesson 11, page 29

1. There are 24 different permutations. The 6 permutations with Oink winning are:
   OBM, OBT,OMB, OMT, OTB, OTM
   There are 6 arrangements for each frog winning first place.
2. A = Alberto, B = Burt, C = Chacha
   ABC, ACB, BAC, BCA, CAB, CBA

Lesson 12 - page 30

1. 24 arrangements
2. 5 x 4 x 3 = 60 possible finishes

Lesson 13 - page 31

1. 6 x 5 x 4 x 3 = 360
2. 6 x 5 x 4 = 120

Lesson 14 - page 32

1. 4 x 3 x 2 x 1 = 24 phone numbers
2. 6 x 5 x 4 = 120

Lesson 15 - page 33

1. 3 x 2 x 1 = 6
2. 4 x 3 x 2 x 1 = 24

Tessellations

Lesson 1 - page 34

Students should draw six triangles and three hexagons tessellating around the points.

Lesson 2 - 14

Answers may vary, but check to see that students have made the correct drawings.

Graphing

Lesson 1 - page 48

1. A - 8	B - 2
C - 13	D - 0
2. E - 4	F - 8
G - 12	H - 10
I - 6	J - 2

Lesson 2 - page 49

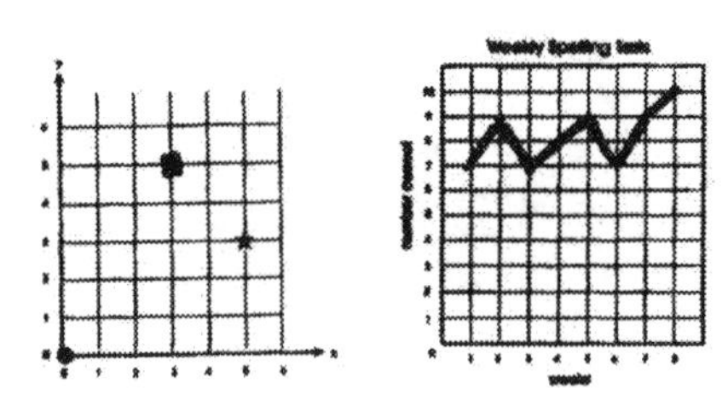

Lesson 3 - page 50

Sweet City - (3, 5)
Heart Lake - (2, 3)
Mt. Cupid - (6, 5)
Honeyville - (8, 2)
Darling Creek/Romance River - (9, 3)
Liebeberg - (2, 2)

Lesson 4 - page 51

(4, 8)	(9, 3)
(5, 10)	(6, 2)
(6, 12)	(3, 1)
(7, 14)	(0, 0)

The graph will show two straight lines that originate at (0,0). One ends at the point (7, 14) and one at the point (15, 5). See firrst graph under Lessons 7-14.

Lesson 5 - page 52

a. -1°	b. -3°
c. -1°	d. -4°
e. -7°	f. -7°
g - o.	

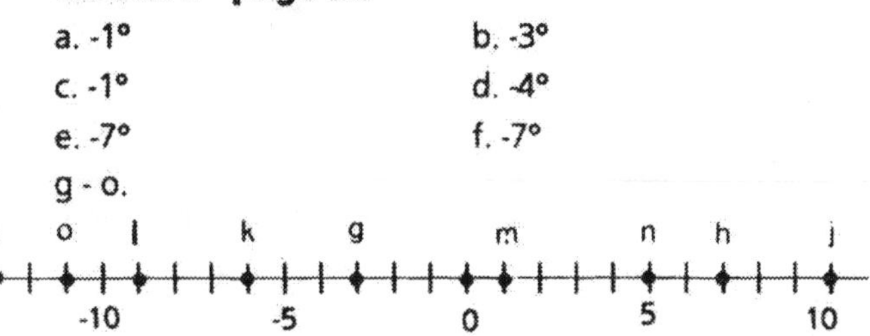

Lesson 6 - page 53

1. (2, 2)	2. (-4, -3)
3. a. 1st	d. 3rd
b. 4th	e. 2nd
c. 2nd	f. 3rd

Lesson 7 - 15

Graphings should produce pictures like the following

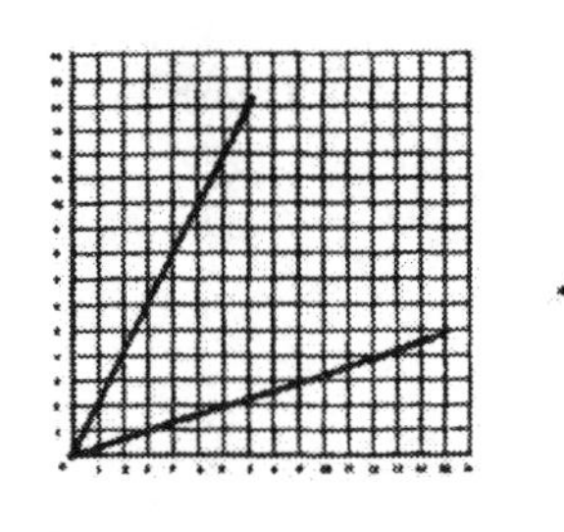

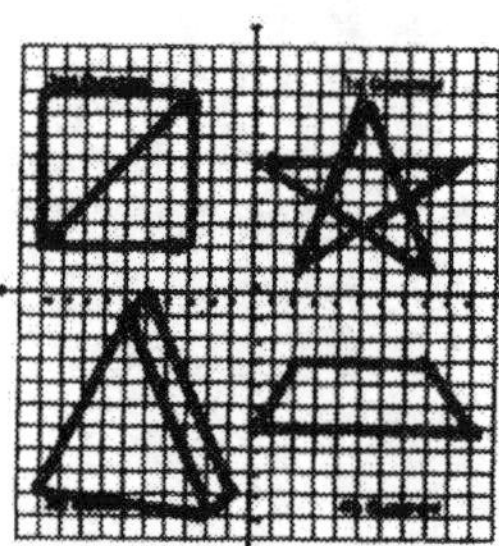

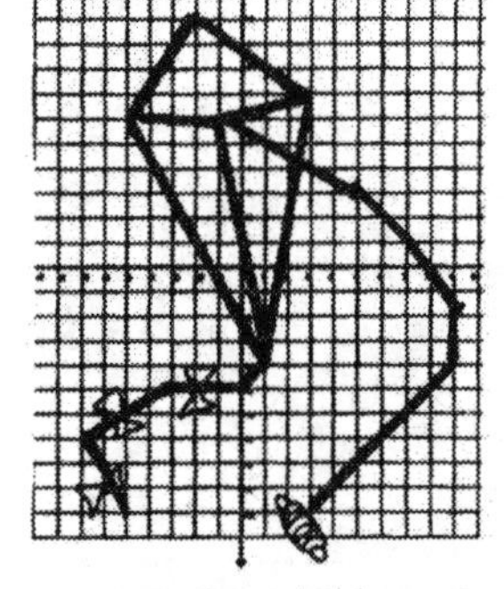

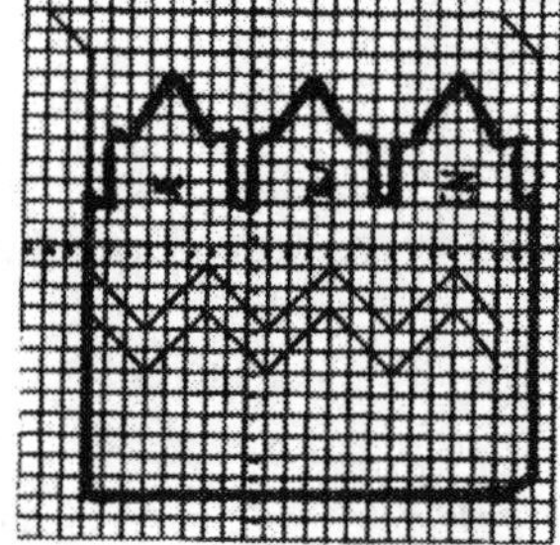

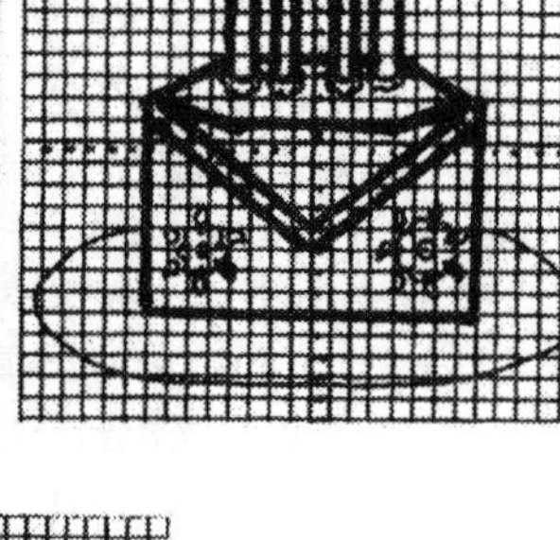

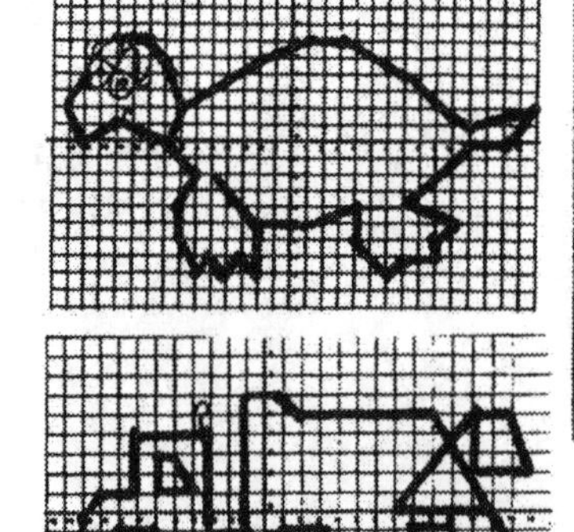

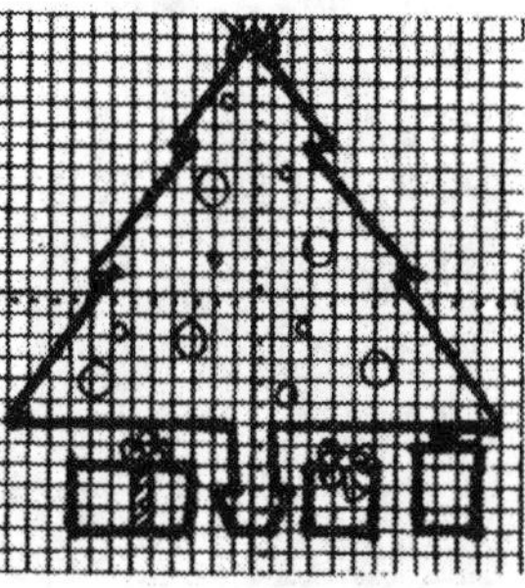

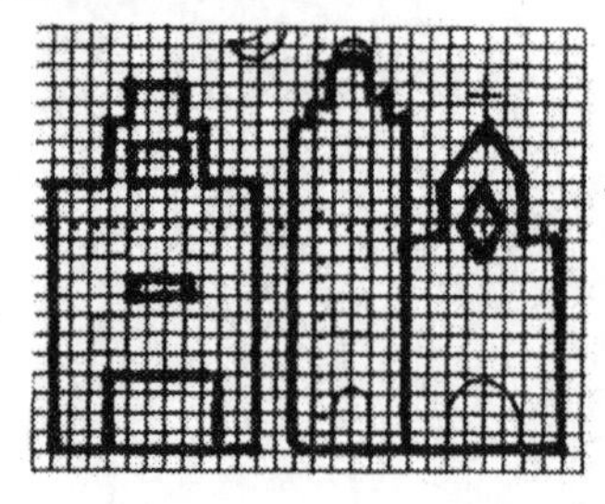

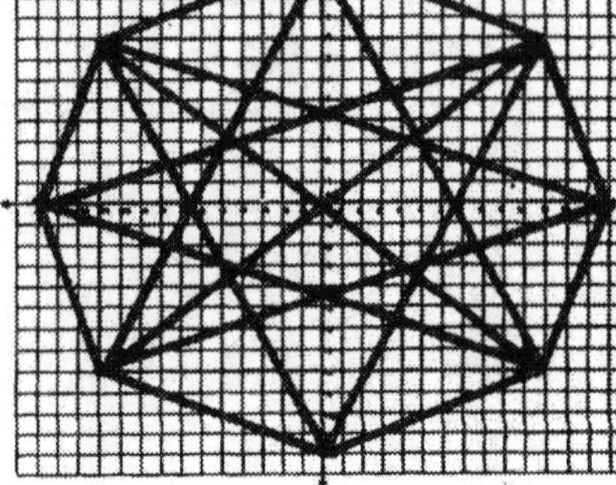

Printed in the United States
by Baker & Taylor Publisher Services